# THERE GOES THE BRIDE

## A FARCICAL COMEDY IN TWO ACTS

### RAYMOND HOPKINS

## HANBURY PLAYS

KEEPER'S LODGE • BROUGHTON GREEN
DROITWICH • WORCESTERSHIRE • WR9 7EE

BY THE SAME AUTHOR:
*LOVE BEGINS AT FIFTY*

## THERE GOES THE BRIDE

FIRST PUBLISHED 2000

by

Hanbury Plays   Keeper's Lodge   Broughton Green
Droitwich   Worcestershire   WR9 7EE

ISBN: 185205 250 3

The author of this play, Raymond Hopkins, is donating his share of the proceeds to
MULTIPLE SCLEROSIS RESEARCH

# CAST IN ORDER OF APPEARANCE

JOHN TAYLOR

About forty-eight. Lets the world go by, henpecked by his wife, loves gardening. Hard worker.

ANNE TAYLOR

About forty-five. Runs the family, but does not like to be put under pressure. Smartly dressed.

JASON TAYLOR

About twenty-five. Only child of John and Anne Taylor. Down to earth, a quiet, deep thinking, romantic person.

STELLA PARSONS

About fifty. Jumped-up snob, plenty of money, but in a loveless marriage. Trying to find a man who will give her affection.

LUCINDA PARSONS

About twenty-five. Only daughter of Stella and Reg Parsons. Emotional wreck, talks with a lisp, has been dominated by her mum. Does not make the best of herself until Act II, Scene II. Then she is transformed. She loses her lisp and looks lovely.

FRED STUBBLE

About sixty-eight. Reasonably well educated. A ladies' man, full of life and is a real character. Acts like a man twenty years younger.

JULIE HEMMINGS

About twenty-two. From poor background. Pretty girl who is kind and considerate.

CHRIS TUCKER

About twenty-five. Quick thinker. Jack-the-lad, anything goes, lives for today. Jason's best friend.

SID BLUNSDEN

About forty-five. Big thinker, full of flannel. Married, without children. Runs his own video recording business.

ALF PRATT

About thirty-five. Dishevelled nerd, who talks out of the back of his head. Lodges with Sid and his wife. Helps with Sid's video business.

REV. ALAN STEVENS

Chris in dog collar with disguise. Suggest beard, glasses, wig or false teeth. Also use different voice and a fictitious actor's name in programme.

NOTES

(1) The whole plot of the play depends on Chris not being recognisable as the Rev. Alan Stevens.

(2) In Act I, Scene I, Anne and Stella must be wearing similar coloured clothes.

THE ACTION TAKES PLACE IN A SMALL TOWN IN THE MIDLANDS.
IT IS SET IN THE LOUNGE OF THE TAYLORS' SEMI-DETACHED
HOUSE. IT IS LATE SPRING – THE PRESENT DAY

ACT I

Scene One – Saturday morning – one week before the wedding

Scene Two – The following Monday – late afternoon


ACT II

Scene One – The following Wednesday – late afternoon

Scene Two – The following Sunday morning

# ACT 1

## ∽ Scene I ∽

*(As the curtain rises, John is sitting in a chair, reading a newspaper. The phone starts to ring. John answers it)*

JOHN          Hello ... hello, Sandra ... yes ... no ... yes ...

*(John holds the phone away from his ear and moves his head from side to side, pretending to talk. Anne enters from kitchen, unseen by John)*

ANNE          What are you doing?

JOHN          Ahh ... *(John faces Anne)* Nothing ... it's your sister. *(Puts hand over phone)* She's upset about the wedding.

*(John hands over phone. Anne glares at him. John sits down and reads paper)*

ANNE          Hello, Sandra ... pardon? ... Look, I agree with you, your daughter should have been asked. Oh, don't be like that ... *(John looks up)* ... just calm down ... *(John reads paper)* ... Sandra ... Sandra ... Sandra? *(Anne puts phone down.)*

I can't believe it, she's hung up. *(Pause)* They're not coming to the wedding.

JOHN          *(Looking up from paper)* Why not?

ANNE          Because Jennifer wasn't asked to be a bridesmaid. *(Pause)* Mind you it's not fair, the six bridesmaids are all from the other side.

JOHN          You make it sound as if they've risen from the dead.

ANNE          Don't be stupid, you know what I mean. What am I going to do?

JOHN          Phone her back and say she can be a bridesmaid.

ANNE          The wedding's next week and Jennifer hasn't got a dress.

JOHN          She could wear that blue one she had for her birthday.

ANNE          Everyone else'll be in *pink*. If she wears blue she'll stand out like a ballet dancer working on a building site.

JOHN          You should have sorted all this out before.

| | |
|---|---|
| ANNE | Lucinda and her mum had chosen all the bridesmaids before I'd realised. |
| JOHN | It's our son that's getting married. Surely we can pick one. |

*(Phone rings)*

| | |
|---|---|
| ANNE | This phone's just not stopped. *(Anne picks up phone, John reads paper)* Hello ... hello, Jack ... I don't know ... can't you take it back? ... Oh I see ... well you did have the wedding list ... bye. |

*(Anne puts down phone. John looks up from paper)*

Jack's found out someone else has bought a toaster.

| | |
|---|---|
| JOHN | He'll have to go back to the shop and change it. |
| ANNE | He didn't buy it from a shop, he got it from a car boot sale. *(Pause)* This wedding's getting too much for me. It's been one crisis after another. |

*(Phone rings)*

| | |
|---|---|
| JOHN | That'll be Jack again. He bought that cheap phone which keeps going into redial mode. |
| ANNE | *(Getting cross)* I've just about had enough. *(Picking up phone)* You've done it again, you pillock! ... Oh, hello, Vicar ... yes, certainly ... we're really looking forward to the wedding ... see you soon ... bye. *(Anne puts down phone)* I think I've just ruined my chances of seeing the pearly gates. |
| JOHN | What did the Reverend Hall want? |
| ANNE | He's calling round Monday to see Jason and Lucinda. *(Pause)* Where's my list? *(Anne looks around room)* |
| JOHN | Your whole life revolves around a list of jobs on a piece of paper. |
| ANNE | That's because although I can remember what I did forty years ago, I haven't a clue what happened yesterday. |
| JOHN | That's nothing to worry about. *(Pause)* It's just part of the ageing process. |
| ANNE | Watch it. *(Anne picks up clipboard with A4 sheet on it)* Ah, here we are. *(Reading from list)* You've got to see your friends about videoing the wedding. |
| JOHN | There's no panic, I'll do that tomorrow. |
| ANNE | *(Looks back at list)* I've got to ring the florist about our buttonholes. |
| JOHN | Don't bother to get me one. I've got some roses in the garden. |
| ANNE | Don't be stupid, you're the bridegroom's father. You'll have one from the florist like everyone else. *(Looking back at list)* I've got so much to do, it's ridiculous. |
| JOHN | Calm down or you'll have one of your power surges. |

| ANNE | Flippant remarks about my hot flushes are in poor taste. |
|------|------|
| JOHN | I've never seen you so uptight. |
| ANNE | It's all right for you sitting there oblivious of everything. |
| JOHN | Weddings are overrated. They're just an excuse for lots of sad people to try and outdo each other in some glorified fashion parade. |
| ANNE | The only sad person is you. You're such a skinflint you'd have the bride arriving on a pushbike, and the reception at *Sloppy Sam's Snack Bar*. *(Phone rings)* You can get that. |
| JOHN | *(Picking up phone)* Hello ... Oh right, that's good ... So it's well rotted ... Thank you. *(John puts down the phone)* They're delivering my manure within the next few days. |
| ANNE | If you put as much effort into your son's wedding as you do that wretched garden you'd ... *(Looking at her list)* I've written down "make love." |
| JOHN | Now that is good news. It's not my birthday is it? |
| ANNE | It's all right ... I remember what it is now. |
| JOHN | I hope you do. Come on, let's go for it before you have another amnesia attack. *(John holds out his hand and heads for hall exit)* |
| ANNE | Come back here, Romeo. *(Pause)* You've got to have a talk to your son about what to do in bed. |

*(John walks back into room)*

| JOHN | Anne, the age of innocence has gone, it's free love for all now. |
|------|------|
| ANNE | Best to be on the safe side. Just make sure he knows what goes where. |
| JOHN | You've only got to turn the telly on, open a magazine, or go to the cinema. It's reached epidemic proportions. |
| ANNE | We don't want his honeymoon to be like ours. That was a total disaster. |
| JOHN | You said you wouldn't mention that again. |
| ANNE | We spent all night doing a jigsaw puzzle of a squirrel. At breakfast next morning, when you said you couldn't find your nuts, everybody laughed. *(Pause)* They didn't know you were on about a lost piece of puzzle. |
| JOHN | Perhaps we could get the vicar to explain what to do. |
| ANNE | Don't be stupid, that's not his job. *(Looking at list)* Now let me see. We've got Lucinda and her mum calling in to make the final arrangements. |
| JOHN | In that case I'll mow the lawns. |

| | |
|---|---|
| ANNE | Oh no you don't. You'll stay here and talk to Stella. |
| JOHN | I can't stand the woman. She's nothing but a jumped-up snob. |
| ANNE | I've got to admit she's going over the top with this wedding. |
| JOHN | It must have cost them at least fifty grand. |
| ANNE | And the rest. *(Pause)* I'll miss Jason when he moves out. *(Pause)* I might get a dog. |
| JOHN | Animals are a big responsibility. A dog's not just for Christmas. |
| ANNE | That's good, because summer's almost here. *(Pause)* It'll be a new interest in life, something for me to shower my affection on. |

*(John puts his arm around Anne)*

| | |
|---|---|
| JOHN | You can always shower your affection on me. Why have a dog when I'm here? |
| ANNE | Because I can put the dog in a kennel at night, when I want to get to sleep. *(John removes his arm from Anne)* |
| JOHN | Umm … *(Pause)* I see your point. |
| ANNE | Have a think about it, and let me know. |
| JOHN | If we do get one, we'll call it *Randy*, just like its master! |
| ANNE | That's a laugh. |
| JOHN | I've got something in my right eye, would you have a look? |
| ANNE | *(Peering into John's eye)* I can't see anything, it's probably some down off that new quilt. |
| JOHN | It's really sore. I can't stop blinking. |
| ANNE | Don't make such a fuss, you big baby. |

*(Jason enters from hall)*

Morning, darling, did you sleep well?

| | |
|---|---|
| JASON | Not too bad, although I kept thinking about the wedding. |
| ANNE | I expect you'll be pleased when the big day's here. |
| JASON | I suppose so, although it all seems to be getting a bit out of hand. |
| JOHN | How long have you and Lucinda been courting? |
| JASON | What do you mean, courting? |
| JOHN | Good grief, I can't be that old, can I? How long have you two been going out together? |

| | |
|---|---|
| JASON | I'm not sure, she always seems to have been hanging around. |
| ANNE | You'd better not let Lucinda hear you say that. |
| JOHN | I'll put some toast on for your breakfast. *(Pause)* Come on, Randy. WALKIES! |

*(John exits to kitchen, pretending to lead a dog)*

| | |
|---|---|
| JASON | Is Dad feeling all right? |
| ANNE | Yes, we've been talking about getting a dog. |
| JASON | Oh, I see. *(Pause)* Just before your wedding, did you have any doubts? |
| ANNE | I think everybody does. After all it's a big decision. |
| JASON | How do you know when you're in love? |
| ANNE | It's no good asking me; I'm married. |
| JASON | But that's just what I mean. How do you know if you've chosen the right person? |
| ANNE | What's brought all this on? Don't tell me you and Lucinda have had a row? |
| JASON | No. It's just me. Last minute nerves and all that. |
| ANNE | Oh, that's good. *(Pause)* How are you getting on with Lucinda's mum? |
| JASON | Absolutely fine *(Pause)* when she's not around. |
| ANNE | Jason, you're talking about your future mother-in-law. |
| JASON | I'll tell you something. She's a man-eater. |
| ANNE | What, Stella? I can't believe that. |
| JASON | It's true. Her husband's lost interest, so she's looking elsewhere. |
| ANNE | Goodness, I'd never have thought that of her. |
| JASON | I think she's trying to re-live her lost youth. |
| ANNE | Aren't we all? |

*(John enters from kitchen)*

| | |
|---|---|
| JOHN | It's in the toaster. *(Doorbell rings)* My eye's still sore. |

*(John exits to hall rubbing his eye)*

*(Off)* Hello, Stella, Lucinda. Come in.

| | |
|---|---|
| STELLA | *(Off)* Hello, John. *(Lucinda, Stella, John enter. Stella is carrying a large picture, which she puts on sideboard)* Well, only one week before my little Lucinda becomes the bride of the year. Hello, Jason. *(Pinches his cheek)* You'll soon be calling me Mother. |
| JASON | I can't wait. |

**9**

| | |
|---|---|
| LUCINDA | Mummy, do you think my wedding photos will be in all the local papers? |
| STELLA | Of course they will, darling. I expect they'll be on the front page. |
| LUCINDA | That's good. *(Pause)* Kim Swanson was interviewed by the local radio on her wedding day. |
| STELLA | Was she? I'll phone and make sure they interview you. |
| JASON | We don't want too much publicity. |
| STELLA | Don't be silly. My Lucinda's going to have the full works. |
| JOHN | *(Aside)* I wish someone would give you the full works. |
| STELLA | We can't stop long. Lucinda's got her final dress fitting. |
| LUCINDA | I hope they've sewn the sequins on, and lengthened the train. |
| STELLA | Don't worry your pretty little head, darling, Mummy will sort it all out. |
| ANNE | Are you pleased with the dress, Lucinda? |
| LUCINDA | I think it's … |
| STELLA | The last time she tried it on, I just wept and wept buckets of tears. |
| JOHN | Was it that bad? |
| STELLA | She looked so beautiful. Just like a princess. |
| JOHN | When I tried my wedding suit on I wept. I couldn't believe it was costing so much. |
| LUCINDA | I hope it won't rain on my wedding day. |
| STELLA | *(Looking up)* It had better not, or I shall want to know the reason why. |
| JOHN | My garden could do with a good soaking. The spuds are no bigger than marbles. |
| STELLA | Your potatoes'll have to wait. I've ordered fine weather for Saturday. |
| LUCINDA | I won't be able to see you tonight, Jason. I've got a beautician and hair stylist calling round for a consultation. |
| JOHN | *(Aside)* Perhaps they can work a miracle on your mum. |
| ANNE | What are you muttering about, John? |
| JOHN | I just said that could be a lot of fun. |
| STELLA | We've got a top hairdresser. He's creating a unique style just for my Lucy Lou. |
| ANNE | I'm sure you'll look absolutely beautiful. |
| STELLA | Now we must sort out the church service … |

| | |
|---|---|
| JOHN | I'll just go and mow the lawns. |
| JASON | My toast should be ready. *(Anne glares at John)* |
| STELLA | That's right, off you pop and leave us girls to make the final arrangements. |
| | *(Jason and John exit to kitchen)* |
| | Now, where were we? Oh yes, last night I had a nightmare about choirboys. |
| ANNE | Choirboys? |
| STELLA | *(Stella goes into a panic)* They were all suffering from laryngitis and couldn't sing a note. |
| ANNE | Oh dear, how awful. |
| STELLA | I phoned the Reverend Hall this morning and told him to bring some spare ones along. |
| LUCINDA | Would it be all right if I got myself a cold drink? I'm feeling a bit flushed. |
| STELLA | Promise Mummy you're not going to be ill. *(Stella puts her hand on Lucinda's forehead)* Have you got a fever? |
| LUCINDA | I did sneeze four times yesterday. |
| STELLA | Oh no! When we get home I'll get the doctor to call round. |
| LUCINDA | All right, Mummy. I'll go and have a chat to Jason. |
| STELLA | Don't get cold, Lucy Lou. |
| | *(Lucinda exits to kitchen)* |
| | That's all I need. Now where was I? Oh, yes. I've told the hire company I want more cars. |
| ANNE | But we've already got three, and a horse and carriage. We could transport a rugby team. |
| STELLA | I've changed it to five cars, plus the horse and carriage. |
| ANNE | I don't really see the point. |
| STELLA | Best to be on the safe side. In any case, that Mrs Ferguson had four cars for her daughter's wedding. |
| ANNE | I've just had a phone call from my sister. They're not coming to the wedding. |
| STELLA | Tell me it isn't because they feel inferior to my family. |
| ANNE | Certainly not. It's because her daughter wasn't asked to be a bridesmaid. |
| STELLA | I'm sure we can work something out. |

**11**

| | |
|---|---|
| ANNE | Thank you so much. It's just that she's always wanted to be a bridesmaid, and I feel …. |
| STELLA | I've got it. *(Looking thoughtful)* The guests will need directing to the loos. *(Looking pleased)* Is that a possibility? |
| ANNE | My niece isn't going to be a lavatory attendant. |
| STELLA | Oh, well, it was just a thought. |
| ANNE | I'm not very happy about this. After all, she is my sister. |
| STELLA | I completely understand how you feel. *(Pause)* We can choose our friends, but we can't choose family. |
| ANNE | So what am I going to tell Sandra? |
| STELLA | Tell her not to worry, we'll soon fill their seats at the reception. |
| ANNE | That's no good. This has put me into an impossible position. |
| STELLA | Did I tell you that I've invited the mayor and his wife? |
| ANNE | I didn't realise you knew them. |
| STELLA | I don't, but it all helps to give the occasion that certain something. They've accepted, and he's told me he'll be wearing his robe and chains. |
| ANNE | Oh, that'll be nice for him. |
| STELLA | He's already given me his wedding present. *(Stella picks up the large abstract picture from sideboard. The picture is random-coloured lines, squiggles, and circles)* Have a look at this. *(Stella hands picture to Anne)* What do you think? |
| ANNE | *(Holding picture upside-down and staring at it)* It looks a bit rude to me. |
| STELLA | You've got it upside-down. *(Anne turns picture up the right way)* He was in an abstract mood when he painted this. It's called *Forgotten Dreams*. |
| ANNE | *(Looking vague)* It's certainly different. |
| STELLA | *(Snatching picture back)* One's got to be in tune with abstract art, to experience its hidden depths. |
| ANNE | If you say so. *(Stella puts the picture back onto the sideboard)* |
| STELLA | I've just had my final meeting with the wedding co-ordinator. I've told him if he doesn't get it right, his job's on the line. |
| ANNE | I wouldn't want to be in his shoes. |
| STELLA | The caterers are pushing their luck. They promised me a top chef from the London Academy, and now we've got some under chef from Luton airport. |
| ANNE | Are you sure we need seven courses? We'll be eating till midnight. |

| | |
|---|---|
| STELLA | Just leave it to me. Everything's organised. *(Pause)* My Reg got so excited last night. *(Pause)* It looked magnificent when it was lit up. |
| ANNE | I beg your pardon? |
| STELLA | The paddock. Reg put all the floodlights on. |
| ANNE | Oh, of course, we're having the reception in a marquee at your house. |
| STELLA | Well, I mean, with our ten acres, it seemed silly to go elsewhere. In any case, the orchestra insisted on perfect acoustics. |
| ANNE | We wouldn't want to upset the orchestra. |
| STELLA | By the way, are you sure these fellows will be all right videoing the wedding? |
| ANNE | Oh yes. John says they're very good. |
| STELLA | I'd much rather hire a professional firm. Money's no object. |
| ANNE | It's the only contribution our family's making. Don't worry, they'll be fine. |
| STELLA | We don't want any slip-ups. It's such an important event. Have you seen their credentials? |
| ANNE | No, I've not had that pleasure. *(Pause)* You don't think you're making too much of this wedding, do you? |
| STELLA | Whatever do you mean? |
| ANNE | We've got two-hundred and fifty guests. The whole town's been put on red alert. All police leave's been cancelled, and you're spending enough money to repaint the Millennium Dome. |
| STELLA | We can afford it. Reg's business is doing very well. Just leave it to me. |
| ANNE | If you're sure. I just thought that … |
| STELLA | Look, Lucinda's our only child. I shan't get another chance. I wanted more children, but Reg was always too busy with his road haulage company. |

*(John enters from kitchen)*

| | |
|---|---|
| JOHN | Where's the can of petrol for the mower? |
| ANNE | I don't know. *(Pause)* Oh, wait a minute, Bill next door borrowed it. |
| JOHN | That's just typical, everything we own, he borrows. I'll go and get it. |
| ANNE | No, you have a talk to Stella. I'll get it. I've got to see Margaret about a recipe. |
| JOHN | *(Pointedly)* Thanks a million. |
| STELLA | Of course, we have a gardener. He's so useful, I couldn't manage without him. |

**13**

| | |
|---|---|
| ANNE | Excuse me for a moment. |

*(Anne exits to hall)*

| | |
|---|---|
| JOHN | Reg must be doing well. I'm always seeing his lorries about. |
| STELLA | He's just taken on five more men. *(Getting excited)* One of them was an Eddie Stobart defector. |
| JOHN | Pardon? |
| STELLA | He got fed up wearing a tie to work. *(Pause)* Yesterday the bank manager took Reg out to lunch to discuss his stocks and shares. |
| JOHN | My bank manager's just had a word with me. |
| STELLA | What about, investments? |
| JOHN | No, my overdraft. Anybody would think they were short of money. |
| STELLA | Oh ... the only problem is, Reg is always working. We've become almost strangers. |
| JOHN | I suppose that's the price of running a successful business. |
| STELLA | I've told him we're not on this earth for long. You've got to have some fun. |
| JOHN | My motto's always been 'Enjoy each day as though it's your last' 'cos one day it will be. |
| STELLA | I wish my husband had your outlook on life. *(Pause)* All work and no play makes Reg a dull boy. |
| JOHN | Still it's nice to be financially secure. |
| STELLA | I'd get more affection if I'd married a cash-dispenser machine. |
| JOHN | I suppose money doesn't buy happiness. It just eases the pain of life. |
| STELLA | Reg has never understood the emotional needs of a woman. |
| JOHN | There isn't a man living who understands the emotional needs of a woman. |

*(Doorbell rings, John exits to hall)*

Excuse me. *(Off)* Hello, Fred, come in.

*(John enters with Fred)*

I don't think you've met Lucinda's mum, Stella Parsons. This is our friend Fred Stubble.

| | |
|---|---|
| FRED | Pleased to meet you. *(They shake hands)* |
| STELLA | I'm sorry, but I can't remember if you're coming to the wedding, Mr Stubble. |
| FRED | You can call me Fred. All the girls do. And yes, I'll be there. |

| | |
|---|---|
| STELLA | That's good, and your wife? |
| FRED | I've lost her; she's gone. |
| STELLA | I am sorry, was it sudden? |
| FRED | You could say that. One morning I got up and found a note saying she'd run off with the milkman. |
| STELLA | Oh, dear, I should think you were devastated. |
| FRED | I was. *(Pause)* He hadn't left any milk. |
| STELLA | You must miss her dreadfully. |
| FRED | Yeah, I do, she was the only one who could work the washing machine. |
| STELLA | Have you heard from her since? |
| FRED | Not a word. I wouldn't have minded, but she took all me bottles of Guinness. Talking of drink, me throat's a bit dry. |
| JOHN | Sorry, Fred, would you like a drop of whisky? |
| FRED | That'll do nicely. |
| JOHN | Would you like a drink, Stella? We've got sherry, gin or whisky. |

*(John and Stella walk over to the drinks cabinet. Fred follows. He looks at Stella's legs)*

| | |
|---|---|
| FRED | *(Aside)* Ohh … what a lovely pair of legs. |
| STELLA | Just a small sherry please. I've already had four glasses of wine with the mayor. |
| FRED | Make my whisky a large one. |

*(John pours out drinks)*

| | |
|---|---|
| JOHN | Cheers! *(They all hold up glasses)* |
| STELLA | |
| | Cheers! |
| FRED | |
| STELLA | To Lucinda and Jason. |
| FRED | And may they *enjoy the fruits of nature*. |

*(They all have a drink)*

| | |
|---|---|
| STELLA | Oh dear, that's gone straight to my head. |
| FRED | That's what comes of mixing your drinks. |
| STELLA | *(Hiccups loudly)* Pardon me! *(Stella has another long drink)* Would you top me up please? It's giving me a warm glow inside. |
| JOHN | Certainly. |

**15**

*(John fills Stella's glass)*

STELLA          I don't normally indulge at this time of day. *(Taking another long drink)* Still, this is a special occasion.

FRED            I don't need a special occasion to have a drink.

*(Stella is getting slightly tipsy)*

STELLA          I could get used to this. *(Stella has another drink)* The trouble is, sherry works like an aphrodisiac on me.

FRED            *(Grabbing the sherry bottle)* Here, have another.

*(Fred fills Stella's glass)*

STELLA          *(Taking a sip)* I must be careful, two drinks and I'm anybody's.

JOHN            Don't worry. *(Aside)* I certainly won't be queuing up.

FRED            That's brought a bit of colour to your cheeks.

JOHN            *(Looking bored)* I hope Anne's not going to be long. I've got to mow the lawns.

*(Stella walks over to some photos on the sideboard and bends over to look at them)*

STELLA          When were these taken?

*(John and Fred join Stella)*

JOHN            *(Looking at photos)* About five years ago.

FRED            *(Looking at Stella's bottom.)* *(Aside)* Ahh ... Very nice indeed. *(Fred pats Stella's bottom, then moves away, leaving John standing by her)*

STELLA          Ohh! ... JOHN really, you do surprise me!

JOHN            Well, perhaps it was a bit longer then.

FRED            I just popped round to see if you need a hand behind the bar at the reception.

STELLA          That won't be necessary. We've hired bar staff.

JOHN            Fred used to work at the Nag's Head.

FRED            I used to have me own special drink called *Fred's Bomb*. *(Pause)* It was guaranteed to blow your brains out! *(Pause)* So, you won't be requiring my services?

STELLA          No thank you, Mr Stubble, I mean Fred. We'll be fine.

FRED            That's good, because I'll be able to get down to some serious drinking.

STELLA          I hope the service won't bring back any painful memories of your wedding.

FRED            No, I'll probably have a laugh at poor Jason getting tied down.

STELLA          *(To John)* Have I shown you our holiday photos?

**16**

| | |
|---|---|
| JOHN | I expect so. I've watched every video and seen all the photos you've got. |
| STELLA | No, you won't have seen these. They only arrived yesterday. |
| JOHN | *(Aside)* Just my luck. |
| STELLA | Reginald and I were on holiday in our villa in the South of France. |
| FRED | They let it all hang out over there, don't they? |
| JOHN | What are you on about, Fred? |

*(Stella bends over sofa and rummages about in her handbag)*

| | |
|---|---|
| FRED | You can check what's on offer before signing your life away. |

*(Fred looks at Stella's bottom)*

*(Aside)* Now that's what I like, a bit of beef on the bone.

*(Fred stands by Stella and pats her bottom, then moves away, leaving John standing by her)*

| | |
|---|---|
| STELLA | Ohh … |
| JOHN | Don't worry if you can't find them. |
| STELLA | I've got them, you naughty boy. I really should be getting cross with you. |
| JOHN | Why? I didn't hide them. |
| STELLA | Obviously our little talk's got you thinking. |

*(Stella gives John a nudge)*

| | |
|---|---|
| FRED | Can I have a look? |

*(Stella hands round photos. John isn't interested. Fred has a good look)*

| | |
|---|---|
| STELLA | The trouble was, Reg spent all week on the phone to his business clients. |

*(Fred is studying the photos)*

| | |
|---|---|
| FRED | *(Aside)* That can join my page three collection. |

*(Fred puts a photo in his pocket)*

| | |
|---|---|
| JOHN | Thank you, very nice. *(John looks bored, he hands photos back)* |
| STELLA | There's one missing. *(Looking at John)* It's the one of me topless. I never realised, John. |
| JOHN | *(Oblivious of what's been going on)* Realised what? |
| STELLA | All the time our youngsters have been together, you've been hiding your inner feelings. |
| JOHN | *(Totally confused)* Sorry? |

**17**

| | |
|---|---|
| STELLA | Don't apologise, I'm just glad it's all out in the open. *(Pause)* Fred, be a dear, pop out to the Merc and get my mobile phone. |

*(Stella hands Fred car keys)*

It's on the back seat.

*(Fred exits to hall. Stella gets close to John)*

Could I have another drink, please?

| | |
|---|---|
| JOHN | Same again? |
| STELLA | Just a small one, I've got to be on my guard with you. |

*(John winks his sore eye several times)*

There's no need to keep winking at me, John. I've already got the picture.

| | |
|---|---|
| JOHN | Oh … that's all down to a bit of fluff. |
| STELLA | You cheeky monkey. |

*(John picks up a bottle in one hand, and a glass in the other. He pours out a drink for Stella)*

| | |
|---|---|
| JOHN | Say when. |
| STELLA | That's lovely. *(Stella goes to take her drink, but knocks glass, spilling some over John's shirt)* Whoops … I'm so sorry. |
| JOHN | Don't worry, it'll wash out. |
| STELLA | Let me sponge it now, then it won't stain. |

*(John is still holding bottle and glass. Stella gets her handkerchief and mops John's shirt)*

| | |
|---|---|
| JOHN | There's no need to go to all that trouble: |
| STELLA | *(Getting close to John)* It's a pleasure. Come here. |
| JOHN | *(Looking bored)* That'll be fine now. |
| STELLA | You've certainly got a good physique. |
| JOHN | That's all down to my gardening. It keeps me fit. |
| STELLA | I like a man with a firm body. |

*(Stella stops mopping shirt)*

| | |
|---|---|
| JOHN | I'm not one to let myself go. *(Glibly)* It keeps the girls interested. |
| STELLA | And to think I've never suspected a thing. |
| JOHN | What are you talking about? |

*(Stella now takes her drink)*

| | |
|---|---|
| STELLA | It's all dropping into place now. At the New Year's fancy dress party you were Robin Hood, and I was Maid Marion. I spent all night trying to keep my honour intact. |
| JOHN | I was just an innocent bystander. |
| STELLA | That's what they all say. *(Pause)* You playboy. I'd not had so much fun in ages. |
| JOHN | That Darth Vader was the real menace, poking his luminous rod everywhere. I'm convinced it was the Reverend Hall dressed up. |
| STELLA | It was five years ago when Reg lost his appetite, and put on loads of weight. |
| JOHN | Surely that's a physical impossibility? |
| STELLA | Well, it's a fact. He's sexually inactive, and fatter than Mr Blobby. |
| JOHN | *(Looking embarrassed)* I don't think you should be telling me this. Best to have a word with Reg. |
| STELLA | I've given up with him. Ours has become a marriage of convenience. |
| JOHN | Oh dear. *(Pause)* So what will you do when Lucinda moves out? |
| STELLA | I'll need a new interest in life. I'm not ready to be a frumpish, frigid, fifty-year-old. |
| JOHN | No, I'm sure you're not. |
| STELLA | I've just had an idea. Reg goes out Friday nights to his road haulage meeting. *(Looking vulnerable, Stella gets very close to John)* I get so bored on my own. |
| JOHN | *(Oblivious of Stella's advances)* You should invite a friend round for a few drinks. |
| STELLA | My thoughts exactly. We've obviously got the same problem; our partners have reached the mid-life switch off. I'm fed up with being starved of love and affection. |
| JOHN | *(Looking vague)* I think I'm missing something here. |
| STELLA | We both are. Have a think about it and let me know. I can be very discreet. |

*(Anne and Fred enter from hall, Stella moves away from John. Fred gives Stella her car keys and her mobile phone)*

| | |
|---|---|
| | Thank you, Fred. |
| ANNE | *(To John)* Here you are. *(Handing over petrol can)* |
| JOHN | There's nothing in here, it was full of petrol when he had it. |
| ANNE | I know. He said sorry but his car had run out, so he had to use it all. |

**19**

| | |
|---|---|
| JOHN | That's typical of him. The last time I loaned him a torch I didn't get it back until the batteries were dead. |
| ANNE | Don't make such a fuss. |
| JOHN | I'm going to put a lock on this can. |
| STELLA | *(To Anne)* Would you like to see Lucinda trying on her dress? |
| FRED | Yes, please, I'd love to. |
| STELLA | Actually, Mr Stubble, I was talking to Anne. |
| FRED | Oh sorry. *(Pause)* I wouldn't get in the way. |
| STELLA | It's a ladies' dress shop, full of half-naked women. |
| FRED | Is it? What are we waiting for? *(Fred walks to hall exit)* |
| JOHN | Leave it to the girls, Fred. |
| FRED | But I'm quite an expert when it comes to ladies' fashion. |
| STELLA | I'll just check it's ready. *(Stella dials number on mobile phone)* Hello, this is Stella Parsons. Could you tell me if my daughter's wedding dress is ready ... That's excellent ... we'll be round shortly ... bye. |

*(Anne bends down behind sofa and fiddles about with a castor)*

| | |
|---|---|
| ANNE | Everything all right? |
| STELLA | Yes, they say it's the most exquisite dress they've ever made. I'll probably burst into floods of tears the moment I see it. |
| JOHN | I'll get Lucinda. *(Aside)* I think I'm going to be sick. |
| ANNE | *(Still behind the sofa)* This castor's still faulty. I thought you were going to fix it. |
| JOHN | I'll do it tomorrow. *(John exits to kitchen)* |
| STELLA | When you buy from Harrods, you don't seem to get any problems. *(Pause)* Can we drop you off anywhere, Mr Stubble? |
| FRED | Are you sure you don't want my opinion on the dress? |
| STELLA | No, thank you, we'll manage. *(Anne stands up)* |
| FRED | In that case, would you drop me at the Nag's Head? |
| ANNE | Surely they won't be open at this time of day. |
| FRED | It's all right, I've got me own key. |

*(Lucinda and Jason enter from kitchen)*

| | |
|---|---|
| STELLA | Have you got your speech ready, Jason? |
| JASON | I'm no good at making speeches. |

**20**

| FRED | I've got some jokes that're guaranteed to make the girls wet their knickers. |
|---|---|
| ANNE | The Reverend Hall hasn't forgiven you for the ones you told at the Christmas party. |
| FRED | He hasn't got a sense of humour. |
| STELLA | Everybody ready? You'd better drive, Lucinda, I'm feeling a bit light-headed. |
| JASON | I'll come and see you off. |

*(Lucinda, Stella, Anne, Jason and Fred exit to hall)*

STELLA *(Off)* I've forgotten my handbag, *(Stella re-enters and knocks handbag off sofa arm, everything drops out. She goes behind sofa and picks up contents, John pokes his head round kitchen door. He thinks it is Anne behind the sofa)*

JOHN You're not still fiddling with that castor. By the way, let's give it a try. *(Pause)* Don't forget, *Randy*'s the name. *(John exits to kitchen) (Off)* WALKIES.

*(Stella picks up her handbag, stands up and smiles)*

STELLA *(To kitchen exit)* All right, Randy. See you Friday.

*(Stella exits to hall. Car drives away. Jason enters. He puts on a tape of romantic music. He sits on chair and reads paper. The door bell rings. Jason exits to hall)*

JULIE *(Off)* Hello, I'm from 'Pinks' the florist. We're supplying the flowers for your wedding.

JASON *(Off)* Really? You'd better come in. *(Jason and Julie enter room)*

JULIE I've called to sort out what buttonholes you require?

*(Jason turns music down low)*

That's one of my favourite songs.

JASON What a coincidence. It's my favourite too.

JULIE I was going to phone, but it seemed easier to pop in and show you what I've got.

JASON I'm glad you did. *(Pause)* I haven't seen you before.

JULIE I've only recently moved. I live in a flat with a friend just up the road. By the way, I'm Julie.

JASON I'm Jason.

*(They look at each other for a few seconds. There is a special look between them)*

JULIE Are you the lucky man?

JASON What do you mean, lucky man?

**21**

| | |
|---|---|
| JULIE | The bridegroom? |
| JASON | Yeah, that's me. |
| JULIE | It must be very exciting – falling in love and getting married. |
| JASON | *(Unconvincingly)* Umm, very. I can hardly wait. |
| JULIE | What sort of buttonholes would you like? |
| JASON | I've no idea. I've never done anything like this before. |
| JULIE | There's a first time for everything. Let me show you what's on offer. |

*(Julie gets out her book)*

Have a look through. *(They both look through book, Jason turns his eyes to Julie as she points out different buttonholes)* Have you seen anything you fancy?

| | |
|---|---|
| JASON | *(Still looking at Julie)* Yes, I most certainly have. |
| JULIE | So which one is it then? *(Jason looks back into book)* |
| JASON | Actually, I'm not too sure. They're all very nice. |
| JULIE | *(Pointing to the book)* That's one of my favourites. *(Pause)* If you've any questions don't hesitate to ask. |

*(Jason looks through book)*

| | |
|---|---|
| JASON | Male or female? |
| JULIE | You've got me there, I don't think flowers have a gender. |
| JASON | No, I mean the friend you live with, male or female? |
| JULIE | Oh, I see. She's a girl I work with. |
| JASON | I'm so pleased. That's great. |
| JULIE | What's great? |
| JASON | *(Pointing to the book)* That rose, it's lovely. *(Pause)* Are you going out with anyone at the moment? |
| JULIE | No, I haven't met anyone I really like. *(Looking at Jason)* I'm sure when the right boy comes along, I'll know. |
| JASON | *(Looking into Julie's eyes)* Yes, it'll be plainly obvious. |
| JULIE | Is that what happened in your case? |
| JASON | *(Unconvincingly)* Not really. I mean, well, we just drifted together. |

*(Julie looks into book)*

| | |
|---|---|
| JULIE | So, which ones do you like? |
| JASON | I can't make up my mind. |

**22**

| JULIE | Why don't I leave the book? Then you can drop it into the shop when you've chosen. |
|---|---|
| JASON | Sounds good to me. So I'll see you Monday? |
| JULIE | Actually, I'm out on the van Monday making deliveries. |
| JASON | Now you've said that, I've just remembered. I'm a bit tied up Monday. |
| JULIE | Perhaps someone else can pop it round. *(Pause)* I really must be going. |
| JASON | Don't go yet. Let me get you a drink. |
| JULIE | Oh, all right. Could I have an orange juice, please? |
| JASON | You can have anything you want. *(Pause)* One orange juice coming up. |

*(Jason pours two orange drinks)*

| JULIE | Have you known your fiancée long? |
|---|---|
| JASON | *(Looking fed up)* It seems like a lifetime. |

*(Jason and Julie drink orange juice)*

| JULIE | In that case, you've obviously chosen the right girl. |
|---|---|
| JASON | *(Looking at Julie)* What makes you say that? |
| JULIE | I don't know. I just thought you must know her very well by now. |
| JASON | Where have you been all my life? I mean, tell me about your past. |
| JULIE | I wouldn't want to bore you with all the details. |
| JASON | It wouldn't be a bore. *(Unconvincingly)* I've always been fascinated with people's backgrounds. |
| JULIE | The last few years haven't been easy for my parents. My dad got made redundant, and then got into financial difficulties. Our house was repossessed. It nearly split their marriage. Anyway, they've moved up north, taking a live-in job with some wealthy aristocrat. So I decided to move here, and do my own thing. |
| JASON | I'm so pleased … I mean, I'm sorry to hear about your parents, but I'm glad you've moved here. |
| JULIE | It's a bit of a struggle, but I get by. |
| JASON | If there's anything I can do to help, please don't hesitate to ask. |
| JULIE | You'll be far too busy with all the excitement of married life. |
| JASON | I don't think so. *(Pause)* I've just had a brilliant idea. Are you going out tonight? |
| JULIE | No, I'm staying in. |
| JASON | In that case, I'll pop the book round to you later. |

**23**

| JULIE | You don't need to go to all that trouble. |
| JASON | It's no trouble. In fact, I've got nothing planned tonight. |
| JULIE | Well, if you're sure … |
| JASON | Yes, I'm absolutely certain. |
| JULIE | All right, I'll see you later. |

*(Julie goes to hall exit)*

| JASON | Just a minute, I don't know where you live. |
| JULIE | How silly of me. Flat 2, 36a Brixham Way. |
| JASON | I know Brixham Way. See you about seven-thirty. |
| JULIE | Bye for now. |

*(Julie exits. Jason turns up the stereo. He has a broad grin across his face. He clenches his fist and punches the air)*

| JASON | *YES!!* |

# ∽ *Curtain* ∽

# ACT 1

## ∽ *Scene II* ∽

*(As the curtain rises, the stage is empty and the doorbell is ringing. John enters from the kitchen and goes to the hall exit)*

JOHN      *(Off)* Oh, hello, Stella, come in.

*(John and Stella enter)*

STELLA      Is Anne here?

JOHN      No, she's next door. Bill's borrowing my drill, he's too tight to buy one himself.

STELLA      So we're all alone.

*(Stella moves close to John)*

JOHN      Yes, I suppose we are.

*(John moves away)*

You've certainly put a lot of work into this wedding.

STELLA      I've planned everything meticulously. It's going to be a day this town will remember for ever.

JOHN      And how's Lucinda?

STELLA      She's just like her mum, ready, willing and able.

JOHN      I suppose when the wedding's over your life'll seem quite dull?

STELLA      That rather depends on you, John. *(Pause)* How have you been feeling since the other day?

JOHN      *(Looking puzzled)* OK, thanks. How about you?

STELLA      Suffering from night starvation, as usual.

JOHN      *(Smiling)* I know just the thing to make you relax.

*(Stella moves close to John)*

**25**

| | |
|---|---|
| STELLA | What are you going to suggest, you little devil? |
| JOHN | A hot milky drink, just before bedtime. It always works with me. |
| STELLA | That's not quite what I had in mind. Still, we've both put our cards on the table. Shall we sit down? |
| JOHN | Yes, certainly. Make yourself at home. |

*(John sits on sofa, and points to a chair for Stella)*

| | |
|---|---|
| STELLA | Thank you. *(Stella moves past chair and sits on sofa by John)* When did you first realise you wanted to try it? |

*(Stella moves close to John)*

| | |
|---|---|
| JOHN | Try what? |
| STELLA | You know. *(Pause)* A 'new interest in life .... RANDY!!'* |

*(Stella puts her hand on John's knee)*

| | |
|---|---|
| JOHN | Oh that. Well with Jason moving out it seemed like a good idea. |
| STELLA | And to think I never suspected a thing. |

*(Stella crosses her legs)*

| | |
|---|---|
| JOHN | It just seemed the right time. Although I'm a bit concerned about the divided loyalties. |
| STELLA | Let's face facts, we're all consenting adults. |
| JOHN | It's quite a commitment. |
| STELLA | Don't forget your motto. 'Enjoy each day to the full.' |
| JOHN | You're absolutely right. Plus the fact it'll be another way of keeping fit. |
| STELLA | I must be honest, that's something I've never considered. |
| JOHN | It's the affection I'm really looking forward to. |

*(John gets up from the sofa to get a drink)*

| | |
|---|---|
| STELLA | That's what most of us are searching for. |
| JOHN | I can see myself now; romping about on the grass, on a spring day. |
| STELLA | Oh John, I'm not sure ... |
| JOHN | Do you know? People say that having a good licking is very therapeutic. |
| STELLA | You certainly don't suffer with any inhibitions, do you? |
| JOHN | There's nothing wrong with that. |
| STELLA | Of course not. It's just that it's been so long. *(Pause)* Things are moving much quicker than I expected. I'm feeling quite flushed. |

**26**

| | |
|---|---|
| JOHN | In that case you'd better have a drink. |

*(Stella rummages about in her handbag and gets out a bottle of perfume, she sprays it all over herself, then puts perfume back into handbag. John brings a drink and hands it to Stella)*

I've filled it with ice, that'll soon cool you down.

*(John sniffs)*

What's that smell?

| | |
|---|---|
| STELLA | It's *Stuck on you.* |

*(John looks at the bottom of his shoe)*

| | |
|---|---|
| JOHN | Is it? I can't see anything. |
| STELLA | No you silly boy, it's the name of my new perfume – *Stuck on You.* Don't you like it? |

*(John sniffs)*

| | |
|---|---|
| JOHN | Well, it's certainly different. |
| STELLA | It turns men wild, it brings out their animal instincts. Don't let's waste any more time with small talk. |

*(Stella lies back on sofa, lips puckered, arms apart, waiting for action. Anne enters)*

| | |
|---|---|
| ANNE | *(Looking at Stella)* Hello, Stella. |
| STELLA | Ahh ... *(Stella jumps up and runs to hall exit)* I must be going ... |
| JOHN | But I thought you'd come round to see Anne. |
| STELLA | I'll see you later. |

*(Stella exits to hall)*

| | |
|---|---|
| JOHN | That woman's cracking up. I reckon she's been on the bottle. |
| ANNE | I expect the wedding's getting to her. She's been so preoccupied with it. |
| JOHN | Well, it must be something, she's been talking rubbish. *(Pause)* I didn't realise you'd told her we'd be getting a dog. |
| ANNE | I haven't mentioned it to anyone. |
| JOHN | You must have, she even knew we're calling it *Randy.* |
| ANNE | Well, I can't remember saying anything. *(Anne looks at her list)* Right now, I've got to go to the supermarket. |
| JOHN | I'll come with you. I could do with a bit of fresh air. |
| ANNE | You can't, you're needed next door. When Bill plugged your drill in, it blew up! |

| | |
|---|---|
| JOHN | WHAT? That idiot destroys everything he touches. He's a walking disaster. |
| ANNE | I said you'd pop round and have a look at it. |
| JOHN | That's it. I'm not lending him anything else. *(Pause)* I suppose I'd better go and see what he's done. |

*(John exits to hall. Anne gets her handbag. Jason enters from hall)*

| | |
|---|---|
| ANNE | Hello, darling, had a good day at work? |
| JASON | Mum, we've got to have a serious talk. |
| ANNE | I can't stop now. I'm just off to the supermarket. |

*(Anne exits to hall, Jason paces up and down the room. The doorbell rings. Jason exits to hall)*

| | |
|---|---|
| JASON | *(Off)* Hello, Chris. Thank goodness you're here. *(Jason and Chris enter)* I've got to talk to someone. |
| CHRIS | Whatever's up? When you rang and said you'd got a problem I thought that ... |
| JASON | I've just met the girl I'm going to marry. |
| CHRIS | I've driven here like a lunatic, to sort out some major crisis, only to be told of your wedding at which I'm the best man. *(Pause)* You prat. |
| JASON | No, you don't understand. I've fallen in love with a ... |
| CHRIS | How sweet. Personally I'm not into all that love rubbish. As long as they can cook, clean and are clued up on the *Kama Sutra*, I couldn't care less. |
| JASON | I'm not marrying Lucinda. I'm in love with another girl. |
| CHRIS | You're having a laugh, aren't you? |
| JASON | I've never been so serious about anything. *(Pause)* Two days ago I met Julie. |
| CHRIS | Julie who? |
| JASON | She's from the local florist, she called round to sort out the buttonholes. |
| CHRIS | So what's that got to do with you calling the wedding off? |
| JASON | We looked through her book. *(Looking dreamy)* But I couldn't make up my mind, so I went to her flat, and when I gazed into her eyes ... |
| CHRIS | Oh, I get it. Your head filled with romantic music, your eyes filled with stars and your heart went into overdrive, pumping blood to parts of your body that even beers can't reach. |
| JASON | Chris, I'm serious. |
| CHRIS | So am I. Now you listen to me. In five days you're marrying Lucinda. It's too late to change your mind. |

| | |
|---|---|
| JASON | I don't care if it's five days or five seconds. *(Shouting)* I'M CALLING THE WEDDING OFF! |
| CHRIS | I feel sorry for you both. You'll break Lucinda's heart; and her mum'll break your neck. |
| JASON | Whatever are we going to do? |
| CHRIS | We're not going to do anything. You've got yourself into this mess, you're on your own. |
| JASON | But we're best mates. We've been through everything together. |
| CHRIS | Don't start laying the guilt trip on me. *(Pause)* Have you given any thought to the consequences of all this? |
| JASON | Of course I have, and that's why we've got to sort things out. |
| CHRIS | Don't keep bringing up the word 'we'. When will you get it into your thick skull it's nothing to do with me? |
| JASON | So you're prepared to condemn me to a loveless marriage? |
| CHRIS | You should have played the field and got all this out your system years ago. |
| JASON | It's no good living in the past, we've got to ... |
| CHRIS | You've had plenty of chance to put it about. But you've always been far too serious. |
| JASON | None of this is helping my present predicament. |
| CHRIS | Why didn't you join the Club 18–30 as a rep? Then you could have partied till you reached the pleasure planet. |
| JASON | Lucinda's mum seemed to have my life organised. Before I knew it she'd got us engaged, and then wedding plans started creeping into the conversation. |
| CHRIS | Hang on. I've just had a brilliant idea. |
| JASON | Thank goodness for that. I knew you wouldn't let me down. |
| CHRIS | Emigrate to Australia. |
| JASON | Look. All I've got to do is tell Lucinda that I'm not going to marry her. |
| CHRIS | That you've fallen in love with another girl. |
| JASON | Yes. |
| CHRIS | And you've spent the last two days gazing into her eyes. |
| JASON | Yes. |
| CHRIS | She'll have to let the two hundred and fifty guests know, and send all the presents back. *(Speaking quickly)* Cancel the photographer, cars, vicar, caterers, orchestra, bar staff, and break the hearts of six bridesmaids. |

**29**

| | |
|---|---|
| JASON | Yes. |
| CHRIS | Best to emigrate. |
| JASON | Yes. I mean no. |
| CHRIS | Why don't you marry Lucinda and have your flower girl as a first reserve. |
| JASON | I'm *not* marrying Lucinda, and that's all there is to it. |
| CHRIS | What's wrong with her, she's got all the right bits, hasn't she? |
| JASON | Of course she has, but there's no sparkle when we're together. |
| CHRIS | You could always give her a squirt of Mr Sheen. |
| JASON | Lucinda'll make someone a lovely wife, but she's not the girl for me. |
| CHRIS | Look, you've only got to learn six words that'll guarantee marital success with any girl. |
| JASON | What six words? |
| CHRIS | Sorry darling, it's all my fault. |
| JASON | Haven't you ever had that incredible feeling when you're close to a very special girl and your whole body starts tingling? |
| CHRIS | What, you mean, when you fancy a bit of nooky? |
| JASON | No, I'm talking about being in love. In my wildest fantasies I never realised such feelings existed. But now I've found the girl of my dreams, I'm not letting her go. |
| CHRIS | This is all getting too heavy for me. |

*(Doorbell rings. Jason exits to hall. Chris sits on sofa)*

| | |
|---|---|
| JASON | *(Off)* Lucinda, come in. Chris and I have got to have a talk with you. |

*(Chris jumps off sofa and goes out kitchen exit)*

| | |
|---|---|
| LUCINDA | *(Off)* What? About the wedding arrangements? |

*(Jason and Lucinda enter)*

Where's Chris?

| | |
|---|---|
| JASON | I'll just get him. *(Jason looks around room, he tries to open kitchen door, but it won't open)* Chris, are you in there? Come out. |
| LUCINDA | What's going on? Are you two playing a joke on me? |
| JASON | It's certainly not a joke. Just bear with me. *(Jason hammers on door)* Chris, open this door. |

**30**

*(The door suddenly flies open and Chris runs out past Jason and Lucinda, pushing both of them out of the way as he exits to hall)*

CHRIS  Must be going, it's been nice knowing you, Jason. Bye, Lucinda.

*(Chris exits to hall, Jason runs after him)*

JASON  Come back here, you coward. I thought you were my mate.

CHRIS  *(Off)* Will you leave me your stereo? Oh, and your watch?

LUCINDA  I knew it. He's getting nervous about being the best man. I said we should have chosen one of my friends from the *Young Farmers Club.*

JASON  Lucinda, we've got to have a serious talk about the wedding.

LUCINDA  That's good. Because I want to talk about the wedding vows.

JASON  What about the wedding vows?

LUCINDA  Mummy's told me not to say 'obey.'

JASON  But it's nothing to do with your mum. In any case something's happened that ... *(Doorbell rings)* Oh no!!

LUCINDA  Perhaps it's Chris come back for another game of hide and seek.

JASON  I knew he wouldn't let me down.

*(Jason exits to hall)*

SID  *(Off)* Hello, we're the video men.

*(Sid enters pushing Alf in a wheelchair. Both are wearing 'film crew' caps, Alf is wearing sunglasses. Attached to one of the chair's handles is a vertical pole, with a flashing light at the top. Halfway down the pole is a spotlight. They also have a cassette player and video camera. Alf is holding another pole, with a microphone hanging from it. Jason enters)*

We're videoing your wedding. We've got a few details to sort out.

JASON  Oh. Well it's not convenient at the moment. Could we phone you later?

SID  It won't take long. In any case we're very busy people. Our card. *(Sid hands over a card to Jason. He looks at it)*

*(To Lucinda)* Don't look so worried, dear, we'll guide you through it.

LUCINDA  I'm not worried at all. In fact, I'm looking forward to it.

*(Alf, who is in the wheelchair, doesn't look too well, he's almost asleep. Sid walks around Lucinda, making a square with his hands and looking through it)*

SID  Hmm, this could be difficult.

LUCINDA  What do you mean difficult?

SID  I'm trying to find your best side.

*(He continues to move around Lucinda)*

**31**

| | |
|---|---|
| LUCINDA | I beg your pardon? |
| SID | You will be wearing a veil, won't you? |
| LUCINDA | Of course I will. Look, instead of wasting time chattering, we should be sorting out the details. |
| SID | You're right, we've got the blushing bride. *(Aside)* Now all we need is Dracula. |
| JASON | Have you videoed many weddings? |
| SID | Many weddings? You're talking to the professionals, mate. We're a household name in the video business. |
| JASON | But I thought you worked with my dad. |
| SID | Well yes, but that's just my spare-time job. |
| LUCINDA | *(To Sid)* What's the matter with your friend? |

*(Alf gets out of chair and unseen by Lucinda, he comes up behind her and puts his hands on her shoulders)*

Ahh …

| | |
|---|---|
| ALF | Don't be nervous, just relax, you'll be safe in our hands. |

*(Alf removes sunglasses. Lucinda jumps)*

| | |
|---|---|
| LUCINDA | You can walk! Why were you in that wheelchair? |
| SID | It's not a wheelchair, it's a dolly. Right, Alf. Let's show these good folks what we're going to do. Now you stand over there. |

*(Sid moves Lucinda to one side of the stage)*

| | |
|---|---|
| ALF | It's my turn to drive. |
| SID | OK. Keep your hair on. I'll go for a take. This'll get your adrenalin pumping. |

*(Sid switches on the lights then sits in the chair. Alf gets hold of the chair handles)*

Walk slowly towards me. Everybody ready? QUIET! WEDDING TAKE ONE. ACTION!!

*(Alf pulls chair backwards across stage. Sid holds camera to his eye and dangles microphone pole over Lucinda's head. Lucinda stands looking in amazement)*

ACTION. ACTION. CUT! The shot's ruined. What's up with you?

| | |
|---|---|
| LUCINDA | *(Looks amazed)* What do you mean? What was I supposed to do? |
| SID | That's the trouble, working with amateurs. Just walk towards me. *(Alf pushes chair back to starting place)* WEDDING TAKE TWO. ACTION. *(Lucinda follows chair as Alf pulls it backwards over Jason's foot, causing Sid to hit Lucinda's head with the microphone pole)* |

**32**

| | |
|---|---|
| JASON | Ahh … |
| LUCINDA | |

ALF — Whoops, sorry. *(He pulls chair off Jason's foot)*

SID — CUT! That's a wrap. *(Pause)* Don't tell me, I can see you're both impressed.

*(Sid switches off the lights)*

ALF — That's what we in the profession call mobile shots. *(Pause)* In church, you'll be following me, pulling Sid in this dolly.

LUCINDA — Are you suggesting that, in front of all the guests, I'll be walking down the aisle, following you, dragging that contraption, whilst your mate's hitting me on the head with that pole?

SID — You shouldn't have been so close.

LUCINDA — I'm not doing that, let's forget the …

SID — This is really going to impress you.

*(Sid has a cassette player attached to the chair. He puts on a tape of Billy Connolly telling a rude joke, followed by laughter)*

That's going on your wedding tape.

LUCINDA — I'm not having people laughing at me as I walk down the aisle.

ALF — No, it's for the speeches, when someone says something funny. *(Alf starts to laugh)* It's called canned laughter.

LUCINDA — I think it's best if we forget the whole thing. We'll get someone else. You see, I don't …

SID — When you're having the wedding photos taken I'll be walking around with the video camera hidden under my jacket.

*(Sid puts video camera into his jacket with the lens poking out)*

LUCINDA — Why would you want to do that?

SID — Background reactions. Things people wouldn't say to your face.

ALF — I normally hide behind the gravestones. Then people can't see me videoing them.

SID — You soon find out who your friends are. We've had some good laughs.

ALF — What, like when we videoed the best man saying the bride looked as fat as a barrel? *(Sid and Alf laugh)*

SID — She didn't speak to him again, after watching the video.

LUCINDA — I'm not having anyone videoed unless they're aware you're doing it.

**33**

| | |
|---|---|
| SID | Why not? That spoils all the fun. |
| ALF | We'll put 'em at the end, in the out-takes. |
| SID | That's where we usually put some shots of the bride in her bra and pants. |
| LUCINDA | WHAT? |
| ALF | I normally visit the bride's bedroom before the wedding, to get a few intimate pictures. |
| SID | It's surprising how that boosts the tape sales. |
| LUCINDA | Oh no, certainly not! You're not videoing me half naked. |
| ALF | When you can't see us, WATCH OUT, 'cause Alf and Sid will be about. |
| LUCINDA | I'm not having that. Jason, tell them. |
| SID | Come on, Alf, we must be going. |
| ALF | See you on Saturday. |
| SID | Don't worry about a thing. Leave it all to us. |

*(Alf gets into chair and they exit to hall)*

| | |
|---|---|
| LUCINDA | I'm not having those idiots videoing my wedding. |
| JASON | Lucinda, we've got to talk about the wedding. |
| LUCINDA | Talk? I'm going home to talk to Mummy. We've got to hire a professional company. |

*(Lucinda exits to hall)*

| | |
|---|---|
| JASON | Come back, Lucinda. I don't want to get married. |

*(Jason sits on sofa and stares into space. John enters from hall with an electric drill)*

| | |
|---|---|
| JOHN | What's up with Lucinda? She's just zoomed off in her car as though she'd seen a ghost. |
| JASON | She's just met your two video mates. |
| JOHN | Oh good. I said they wouldn't let you down. |
| JASON | Dad, we've got to have a very serious talk. |
| JOHN | I'm sorry, but it's going to have to wait, that idiot next door has just blown up my electric drill. |
| JASON | But it just can't wait. |
| JOHN | Don't tell me you're worrying about your honeymoon. I'll explain everything later. |

*(John exits to kitchen)*

| | |
|---|---|
| JASON | DAD, WAIT, I NEED TO TALK NOW! |

*(Jason sits looking into space for a few seconds, doorbell rings, Jason exits to hall)*

*(Off)* Julie! Come in.

*(Julie and Jason enter from hall)*

| | |
|---|---|
| JULIE | Thank you for yesterday, I had a lovely time. *(Pause)* So what have you been at today? |
| JASON | I was just deciding what to pack. |
| JULIE | *(Looking sad)* I see, what, ready for your honeymoon? |
| JASON | No, I'm thinking of emigrating. It seems to be my only option, now I've met you. |
| JULIE | Oh dear. I think I'd better go. |

*(Julie walks to hall exit)*

| | |
|---|---|
| JASON | No, don't go. You're the only person making any sense at the moment. |
| JULIE | I don't want to cause you any more trouble. |

*(Jason walks over to Julie)*

| | |
|---|---|
| JASON | The last two days have been the best in my whole life. |
| JULIE | Oh, Jason, I was hoping you'd feel the same as me. |

*(They kiss. Jason puts his arms around Julie)*

I never realised what love was, until I met you. I can't bear it when we're apart.

| | |
|---|---|
| JASON | That's all I wanted to hear you say. Now I'm certainly not marrying Lucinda. |
| JULIE | What shall we do? I'm scared. |
| JASON | I'm not scared. *(Pause)* I'm petrified. I've got to talk to Lucinda and sort things out. |
| JULIE | Whatever will her mum say? |
| JASON | I don't think she'll say much. *(Pause)* She'll be too busy trying to kill me. |
| JULIE | Whatever happens, we'll face it together. *(They kiss)* Oh, Jason, I love you, so much. |

*(They kiss passionately)*

| | |
|---|---|
| REV. STEVENS | *(Off)* Hello, may I come in? |

*(Rev. Stevens enters from hall. Jason and Julie jump apart)*

I'm sorry, but the door was open.

**35**

| | |
|---|---|
| JASON | *(Looking embarrassed)* We were just … |
| REV. STEVENS | Yes, I thought you were. Please, let me introduce myself. I'm the Reverend Alan Stevens. Now, you must be Jason? |
| JASON | That's right, but where's our own vicar, the … |
| REV. STEVENS | And obviously this is the young lady you're very much in love with. |
| JASON | So where's the Reverend Hall? |
| REV. STEVENS | I've bad news for you. He's had a motorbike accident and broken both legs. He won't be able to marry you. |
| JASON | *(Jason hugs the Rev. Stevens)* That's wonderful! |
| REV. STEVENS | What, that the Reverend Hall's broken both legs? |
| JASON | No. I'm sorry. I mean … is he going to be all right? |
| REV. STEVENS | They've said he'll make a full recovery, but he's got to spend two weeks in hospital. |
| JASON | What perfect timing. I couldn't have planned things better myself. |
| REV. STEVENS | That's not quite the response I was expecting. |
| JASON | Let me explain. You see, I don't want to get married. It's all been a dreadful mistake. |
| REV. STEVENS | *(To Julie)* Oh dear, you must be devastated hearing all this. |
| JULIE | No, I'm just over the moon. *(Julie hugs the Rev. Stevens)* |
| REV. STEVENS | I'm getting very slightly confused here. |
| JASON | We've been looking for a way out, and now everything's falling into place. |
| JULIE | Thank you so much. *(Julie hugs the Rev. Stevens)* I could kiss you. |
| REV. STEVENS | Oh well, if you must. *(Rev. Stevens stands waiting for a kiss. Julie kisses him)* So are you both saying you want the wedding called off? |
| JASON | Yes, please. Oh, this is too good to be true. *(Jason goes to hug the Rev. Stevens but the Rev. Stevens kisses Julie instead)* |
| REV. STEVENS | You've certainly left things a bit late. |
| JULIE | We realise that, *(Julie hugs Jason)* but our future happiness depends on it. |
| JASON | You'll be condemning me to a lifetime of misery if you don't call it off. |
| REV. STEVENS | Well, if you're sure, we'd better make the arrangements. |
| JULIE | This is the best news I've ever had. |

*(Jason and Julie kiss passionately)*

| | |
|---|---|
| REV. STEVENS | Enjoys kissing, but doesn't want to marry. I've lost all contact with the youngsters of today. |
| JASON | Let's have a drink to celebrate. |
| REV. STEVENS | I thought we'd covered every eventuality in training college. But this is certainly a new one on me. |
| JASON | What would you like? Sherry, whisky, gin? |
| REV. STEVENS | Oh, no, I'm TT. |
| JASON | I beg your pardon? |
| REV. STEVENS | I only drink tea. *(Rev. Stevens gets a tea bag out of his cassock and hands it to Jason)* I carry a bag in case of emergency. |
| JULIE | Would you like me to make it? |
| JASON | Yes please, and make mine a large one. |

*(Jason hands tea bag to Julie, she exits to kitchen)*

| | |
|---|---|
| REV. STEVENS | Could I use the little room, please, only I've a slight bladder problem? |
| JASON | Yes. It's through that door, first right. |

*(Rev. Stevens exits to hall. Phone rings. Jason answers it)*

Hello ... Hello, Jack ... Oh, right, so you've managed to get a kettle ... it just needs repairing ... I see ... well hang onto it, I think the wedding's off ... Yes, off ... I'll explain later ... bye.

*(Jason puts down phone, doorbell rings)*

What now? *(Jason exits to hall)*

*(Off)* Stella? Lucinda?

*(Stella and Lucinda enter, followed by Jason)*

What are you doing here?

| | |
|---|---|
| STELLA | We're not having those stupid videomen. My little Lucinda's been in floods of tears. |
| JASON | Lucinda, you and I have got to talk. |
| STELLA | There's nothing to talk about, I knew I should have booked a professional company. |

*(Jason pushes Lucinda and Stella to hall exit)*

| | |
|---|---|
| JASON | Why don't you take your mum back home, and I'll be round in a minute? |
| STELLA | We're not going anywhere until I've sorted out this wedding video. |
| JASON | Lucinda, we've got to discuss the wedding. You see I ... |

| STELLA | Pop out to the Merc and get my mobile phone, dear. It's on the back seat. I'll soon book a competent firm. |
|---|---|

*(Lucinda exits to hall)*

|  | I don't know what your father was thinking of. |
|---|---|
| JASON | Why don't you have a word with him? *(Looking guilty)* He's in the bedroom. |
| STELLA | Is he? Right. We've got a few things to sort out. |

*(Stella exits to hall. Jason runs to kitchen just as phone rings. Jason picks it up)*

| JASON | Hello Jack ... Oh, so it's gone into redial mode ... Yes, the wedding's still off ... I've got to go ... I'll speak to you soon, ... bye. |
|---|---|

*(Jason puts phone down and runs to kitchen exit, just as Lucinda enters from hall with phone)*

| LUCINDA | Where's Mum? |
|---|---|
| JASON | She's in the bedroom with my dad. Why don't you join them? |
| LUCINDA | Pardon? |

*(Loo flush off)*

| JASON | They're sorting out the wedding video. |
|---|---|
| LUCINDA | Oh, right. I'll pop up. |
| JASON | That's good. Take your time. I mean, we've had some more presents. Have a look at them. |

*(Phone rings)*

| LUCINDA | Are you getting excited about the wedding? |
|---|---|
| JASON | You know me. The original Mr Cool. I'll just get the phone. |

*(Lucinda exits to hall. Jason answers phone)*

|  | Not now Jack, I haven't got time ... Yes, take the kettle back and see if you can get a refund ... bye. |
|---|---|

*(Jason leaves phone off the hook. He runs to kitchen exit just as the Rev. Stevens enters from hall)*

| REV. STEVENS | What a blessed relief. |
|---|---|
| JASON | *(Walking over to Rev. Stevens)* Is that supposed to be a joke? |
| REV. STEVENS | Is everything all right? |
| JASON | Oh, yeah. Things couldn't be better. *(Pause)* Would you just bear with me for a minute? |

*(Jason runs to kitchen exit just as Stella enters from hall with her mobile phone)*

**38**

| | |
|---|---|
| STELLA | He's not up there. |
| JASON | *(Turning round)* Oh dear. I must have misheard what he said. |
| REV. STEVENS . | Hello. I'm the Reverend Stevens. |
| STELLA | Stella Parsons. The bride's mother. |
| REV. STEVENS | You must be very proud of your daughter. |
| | *(They shake hands)* |
| STELLA | Yes I am. *(Pause)* Where's the Reverend Hall? |
| REV. STEVENS | I'm afraid he's had a motorcycle accident. He's in hospital with two broken legs. |
| STELLA | The stupid man. So what's he going to do about my daughter's wedding? |
| JASON | I've just suggested we postpone it. |
| STELLA | WHAT? For one minute I thought you said postpone the wedding. |
| JASON | I did ... er ... as a sign of respect for the Reverend Hall. |
| STELLA | He's not dead, is he? I've never heard such rubbish. |
| REV. STEVENS | I really think we should let the youngsters decide. After all, they're the ones getting married. |
| STELLA | I'm telling you here and now, there's just no way that my daughter's wedding will be postponed. |
| JASON | But in the circumstances, it doesn't seem right. |
| STELLA | Don't be ridiculous, I'll phone the Bishop, and get a replacement. |
| REV. STEVENS | That won't be necessary. If the wedding goes ahead, I shall officiate. |
| STELLA | Oh. Well, I suppose you vicars are all the same. Just make sure you don't fluff your lines. |
| | *(Lucinda enters from hall)* |
| REV. STEVENS | Hello. *(Stella tries to introduce Lucinda to the Rev. Stevens)* |
| STELLA | Of course you two haven't met, I'd like to introduce my dau ... |
| JASON | *(Getting hold of Lucinda)* I don't feel too well. I need some fresh air. Let's go for a walk. |
| | *(Jason runs to hall exit, Lucinda pulls him back)* |
| LUCINDA | Not until we've sorted out this wedding video. |
| JASON | I want to go now. Please come with me Lucinda. |

**39**

| | |
|---|---|
| STELLA | You've probably got pre-wedding nerves, sit down for a minute. |
| | *(Jason starts to pace up and down room)* |
| | I assume the Reverend Stevens will want to talk to you both. |
| JASON | Would anyone like a cup of tea? I'll go and get one. |
| | *(Jason runs to kitchen exit)* |
| STELLA | Nobody wants a cup of tea. Come back here. |
| REV. STEVENS | I'd still like mine, please. |
| LUCINDA | Jason, whatever's up with you? You're like a cat on hot bricks. |
| | *(Jason runs over to Lucinda)* |
| JASON | I must talk to you, Lucinda. Let's go somewhere private. |
| | *(Jason pulls Lucinda to hall exit)* |
| REV. STEVENS | I'm sorry, but I'm very confused. |
| JASON | That makes two of us. |
| REV. STEVENS | Is the wedding on, or is it off? |
| STELLA | ON! |
| JASON | OFF! |
| STELLA | ON! |
| | *(Lucinda pulls Jason back into room)* |
| LUCINDA | Whatever's going on? Where's the Reverend Hall? *(To Stella)* Mummy, why did Jason say the wedding's off? |
| STELLA | The Reverend Hall can't take the service, he's broken his legs. |
| REV. STEVENS | It was a motorcycle accident. |
| STELLA | He shouldn't have been riding the thing. *(Pause)* I suppose he's another of these men going through the mid-life crisis. |
| LUCINDA | So, who's taking the service? |
| REV. STEVENS | If the wedding goes ahead, I shall officiate. |
| STELLA | There's no 'if' about it, the wedding will go ahead. |
| JASON | Isn't it time you went home and got Reg some dinner? |
| STELLA | Are you trying to get rid of me? |
| JASON | *(Getting hold of Lucinda's hand)* I must talk to you. It's very important. Come with me. *(Jason pulls Lucinda to hall exit. Julie enters from kitchen with three cups of tea on a tray)* |

JULIE          I've made the tea.

REV. STEVENS   Ah, now we can sort everything out.

*(Jason lets go of Lucinda, runs over to Julie, takes tray, gives it to Stella then pulls Julie to the hall exit. Everyone looks on in amazement)*

JASON          Come on, Julie. *(Pause)* Lucinda. I'm sorry. The wedding's off!

*(Jason and Julie exit. Stella drops tray on floor. It makes a loud crash)*

# ❦ *Curtain* ❦

# ACT II

## ∞ Scene I ∞

*(As the curtain rises, Lucinda is sitting in a chair. She is clutching Jason's photo and crying pathetically. Stella is pacing up and down the room and Anne is sitting in another chair staring into space)*

STELLA      So you're telling me you've no idea where he is?

ANNE      He's not been in contact. His bed's not been slept in. I'm worried.

LUCINDA      *(Crying)* What's going to happen, Mummy?

*(Stella walks over to Lucinda and puts her arms around her)*

STELLA      I'll tell you what's going to happen. When I get my hands on that boy, I'll do things that'll bring tears to his eyes.

ANNE      I don't think we should lose our tempers. We're all a bit upset at the moment.

STELLA      And to think my Lucinda could have had the pick of any boy she wanted.

LUCINDA      *(Crying pathetically)* I just want my Jason. *(Looking at photo)*

STELLA      Why she had to choose a no-hoper like your son, I'll never know.

ANNE      Hang on a minute. I'm not having you talking about Jason like that.

STELLA      It's the truth. *(Pause)* Or have you a plausible explanation why he ran off with that girl?

ANNE      Well, I don't really …

STELLA      He's broken my Lucinda's heart. He's got to pay for that.

*(Lucinda cries loudly)*

ANNE      He obviously needed time to decide about getting married.

STELLA      We're three days away from the wedding. Don't you think he's left it a bit late?

ANNE      I suppose he should have sorted things out before.

**42**

| | |
|---|---|
| STELLA | That Reverend Stevens knew more than he was letting on. |
| ANNE | I'm sure there's a simple explanation to all this. |
| STELLA | The simple explanation is, your irresponsible son's run off with some girl who's supposed to supply flowers, not personal services to the bridegroom. |
| LUCINDA | *(Wailing)* Ahh ... where is he, Mummy? |
| STELLA | *(Stella pats Lucinda's head)* There, there, Lucy Lou, don't worry. |
| LUCINDA | Why doesn't he ring? |

*(Stella gets very cross)*

| | |
|---|---|
| STELLA | Ring, I'll ring his bleeding neck! |
| LUCINDA | *(Lucinda blows her nose)* Brrr ... I can't stop crying. |
| STELLA | I'll make him understand that no-one, but no-one, messes with me. *(Pause)* I suppose I should have guessed. They say 'like father, like son.' |
| ANNE | What do you mean by that? |
| STELLA | I wasn't going to say anything. I was hoping he'd lose interest. |
| ANNE | Lose interest? |
| STELLA | Your husband's not happy with just one woman. He can't keep his hands off me. |
| ANNE | *What?* |
| STELLA | Ask him. Whenever he's around, he's always trying to force himself on me. It's so embarrassing. |
| ANNE | I don't believe it. You must be mistaken. |
| STELLA | I happened to mention that Reg goes out Fridays and your husband's eyes lit up like spotlamps. |
| ANNE | What, you mean he ...? |
| STELLA | Yes, he said he'd be straight round and it wasn't the nine o'clock news he was hoping to turn on. |
| ANNE | You can't be talking about John. |
| STELLA | I certainly am. Ask him about the photo he's stolen of me, topless on holiday. |
| ANNE | This is all too much. They're both at it. The lecherous louts! |
| STELLA | Of course, I didn't succumb to his advances. Fortunately I'm used to dealing with frustrated men. But a lesser woman may have fallen foul. |

*(John enters from kitchen)*

**43**

| | |
|---|---|
| JOHN | Is there any news? |
| ANNE | Yes. You've been trying it on with Stella. *(Anne walks over to John and slaps his face)* |
| JOHN | Ouch! *(Pause)* What are you on about? I'm not that desperate! |
| | *(Stella slaps John's face)* |
| | Ouch! ... That hurt. |
| ANNE | And to think I've given you the best years of my life. |
| STELLA | I can see you have. |
| | *(Anne looks at Stella then slaps John's face again)* |
| JOHN | Ouch! ... Will you two stop hitting me. |
| ANNE | You gigolo! You're nothing but a wolf in sheep's clothing. |
| JOHN | Have you gone completely mad? |
| ANNE | I must have been mad to marry you. And to think Jason's going to be just the same. |
| JOHN | I hope he is. He's my son and I'm proud of him. |
| ANNE | You know what I mean. He's not happy with one woman. |
| JOHN | Have you two been hitting the bottle? |
| STELLA | Where's my photo? I expect it's already faded where you've been drooling over it. |
| JOHN | What photo? |
| STELLA | Friday nights – mean anything? Who's begged to come round for a drink, and whatever else is on offer whilst Reginald's out? |
| ANNE | It's pitiful for a man of your age. Next you'll be wearing a dirty old raincoat. |
| JOHN | I haven't got a clue what you're talking about. |
| STELLA | Typical of a man. Deny everything, thinking he'll get away with it. You've got the hots for me. |
| JOHN | I'm not even lukewarm when you're around. |
| STELLA | Just listen to him. Butter wouldn't melt in his mouth. |
| JOHN | I don't know what's going on, but I can assure you there's been a misunderstanding. |
| STELLA | Don't come the innocent. Only the other day on that very sofa you were fantasizing over some perverted acts. |
| JOHN | For the last time, will you listen to me? I haven't done anything. |

| | |
|---|---|
| ANNE | So are you telling me you've not made advances to Stella? |
| JOHN | Of course I haven't. The thought's never crossed my mind. |
| STELLA | He's bound to say that. He's hardly going to admit that he finds me sexually irresistible. |
| LUCINDA | What about me, Mummy? |
| JOHN | I haven't been anywhere near your daughter either. |

*(Doorbell rings)*

| | |
|---|---|
| ANNE | We'll sort this out later. I've got far too much on my mind at the moment. |
| JOHN | And I always thought a man was innocent until proved guilty. |

*(John exits to hall)*

*(Off)* Hello, Fred. Come in.

*(John and Fred enter from hall)*

| | |
|---|---|
| FRED | Hello all. I hear young Jason's chickened out. When are we getting our presents back? |
| LUCINDA | Stop them, Mummy. They're all laughing at me. |

*(Stella goes over to Lucinda and puts her arms around her)*

| | |
|---|---|
| STELLA | No-one's laughing at you, dearest. *(Looking into room)* Not if they've got any sense. |
| LUCINDA | What shall I do? What's going to happen to me? |
| STELLA | You're getting married in three days, just as we've arranged. |
| FRED | Who's she marrying then? |
| STELLA | *(Calmly)* She'll be marrying Jason, of course. |
| FRED | But he's run off with another girl. |
| LUCINDA | Mummy, stop him. *(Pathetically)* Why have you forsaken me, Jason? |
| FRED | You should phone a dating agency and see if they can find a last minute replacement. |
| STELLA | Suggestions like that are in very poor taste, Mr Stubble. |
| FRED | I was only trying to be helpful. |
| STELLA | That's the sort of help we can do without. |
| FRED | When the wife left, I joined a dating agency. They kept sending me thirty-year-old girls, it was lovely! |
| STELLA | *(Looking bored)* How very interesting. |

**45**

| | |
|---|---|
| FRED | They crossed me off their books for lying about my age. I'd told them I was thirty-five. |
| ANNE | You men are all the same. |
| FRED | Any chance of a drop of gin? |
| ANNE | The glasses are in the kitchen. They'll need washing. *(Looking at John)* Well ... off you go. |

*(John exits to kitchen)*

| | |
|---|---|
| STELLA | I'll check with Reg to see if there's any news. |

*(Stella picks up a piece of paper, then speaks into a CB microphone)*

*Ice Maiden* to *Road Hog*, have you got your ears on?

| | |
|---|---|
| ANNE | What on earth's that? |
| STELLA | It's a CB. If I press this button I can talk to Reg. He's given all his drivers a picture of Jason and he's offering a thousand pounds reward to the man who apprehends him. |
| ANNE | Anybody would think a murder's been committed. |
| STELLA | There's still a chance that could happen. |

*(Stella speaks into CB microphone and reads from piece of paper)*

*Ice Maiden* to *Road Hog*, have you got your ears on?

| | |
|---|---|
| FRED | *(Looking at Anne)* That's CB talk. It's what the truckers use. |
| STELLA | Reg has given me a list of CB phrases, so that I can talk to the drivers, to find out if they've seen Jason. |
| FRED | I used to have a CB till some *Good Buddy* smashed my rig for chatting up his wife. |
| ANNE | This is all very unnecessary. I'm sure Jason'll be home soon. |
| FRED | Yeah, but will it be in time for his wedding? |
| LUCINDA | Ahh ... *(Lucinda blows her nose)* I'm already on my fourth box of tissues. |
| FRED | Last night in the pub, they were having bets on whether the marriage would take place. I could make a few quid. |
| LUCINDA | Ahh ... I'll never be able to show my face at the *Young Farmers* again. |
| STELLA | I just need five minutes alone with your son. I'd soon make him realise his responsibilities. |
| ANNE | Please, Stella. Let's try and remain calm, so that we can sort things out. |
| STELLA | *(Speaking into CB microphone)* *Ice Maiden*, anyone for a copy. |
| VOICE ON CB | *Ice Maiden*, you've got the *Road Hog*, you're hitting me wall to wall. |

**46**

| | |
|---|---|
| STELLA | *(Speaking into CB microphone)* That's a big ten four. Have you seen Jason, *Good Buddy*? |
| VOICE ON CB | Negatory, but will keep on trucking, Roger Dee, over and out. |
| ANNE | What are they talking about? |
| STELLA | They've not found him yet, but they're still looking. |
| ANNE | Why don't they talk plain English? |
| FRED | It's to confuse the police. |
| ANNE | Why bother? The police get confused if you ask them the time. |

*(Stella puts down microphone and John enters from kitchen with glasses and pours out drinks)*

| | |
|---|---|
| JOHN | Here you are, Fred. |
| STELLA | I'll have a sherry. It might help to settle my nerves. |
| ANNE | And me. I've got a hot flush coming on. |
| JOHN | *(Aside)* Not another power surge. *(Pause)* Lucinda? |
| LUCINDA | I couldn't drink a thing. I just want my Jason back. |

*(John hands round drinks)*

| | |
|---|---|
| FRED | Cheers, everyone! *(Fred holds up glass)* The bride and groom. *(Pause)* Wherever he may be. |
| LUCINDA | Ahh ... Mummy. He's making fun of me. |
| STELLA | Mr Stubble. Please think what you're saying. |

*(They all drink. Doorbell rings)*

| | |
|---|---|
| FRED | That could be Jason, forgotten his key. |
| JOHN | I'll go. |

*(John exits to hall)*

*(Off)* You'd better come in. You've upset Lucinda and her mum.

*(Lucinda jumps out of her chair and runs to hall exit)*

| | |
|---|---|
| LUCINDA | He's come back, I knew he would. Jason ... |

*(John enters, followed by Sid carrying a video camera and Alf carrying a microphone tied onto a pole)*

Oh no, Mummy, it's those horrid videomen.

| | |
|---|---|
| SID | What's up then? Hasn't the wanderer returned? |
| ALF | Perhaps he's not ready to start his life sentence! |

**47**

*(Sid nudges Alf, they both laugh)*

| | |
|---|---|
| STELLA | I don't find your stupid remarks at all funny. |
| SID | We could always video the divorce for you. All part of the service. |
| STELLA | I've been desperately trying to hire a professional company, but they're all booked up. |
| ALF | There's no need to take it out on us just because your daughter's been dumped. |
| LUCINDA | Mummy ... have I been dumped? |
| JOHN | I'm sure Sid and Alf will make an excellent job of videoing the wedding. |
| FRED | That's if there is one! |
| JOHN | Who'd like a top up? |

*(John goes around with the drinks)*

| | |
|---|---|
| STELLA | These should have been the happiest days of Lucinda's life. But thanks to your stupid son, she's facing the world on her own. |
| LUCINDA | Why's he left? What's wrong with me? |
| SID | It's not your fault. *(Aside)* Mother Nature's got to take some of the blame. |
| ALF | Jason shouldn't have gone off like that. He was totally out of order. |
| STELLA | That's the first intelligent thing you've said. |
| ALF | Well, I mean, if he don't turn up, we'll have to cancel the stag-night. |
| SID | This is serious. We've got that erotic dancer coming, with her pet python. |
| ALF | We can't cancel that, we'll have to carry on without him. |
| SID | Yeah, we'll drink to absent friends. |
| STELLA | My daughter's sitting there breaking her heart, and you're worried about a stupid stag-night. |
| SID | We were lucky to get Lusty Linda. Her pet python should be paid a fortune for what he has to do. |
| ALF | *(Aside)* I'd do it for nothing. |
| STELLA | It's difficult to believe that morons like you are part of the human race. |
| ALF | Strikes me Jason had a lucky escape from having you as a mother-in-law. |
| JOHN | Drink up, everybody. Here Stella let me top you up. |

*(John goes over to Stella with sherry bottle)*

| | |
|---|---|
| LUCINDA | Will I be wearing my wedding dress on Saturday, Mummy? |

| | |
|---|---|
| ALF | Of course you will. *(Pause)* You can put it on when you go to the chippy for your dinner. |
| SID | I've heard he's emigrating. |
| ALF | I bet he's on some beach with that bird, having a snog. |
| LUCINDA | Stop them, Mummy. This is all getting too much for me to bear. |
| ALF | Still, every cloud's got a silver lining. *(Pause)* It's happy hour at the 'Nag's Head' Saturday. You'll be able to drown your sorrows for half the price. |
| STELLA | That's it, I've had just about enough of this. |
| ANNE | What lovely weather we've been having lately. |

*(Stella gets cross)*

| | |
|---|---|
| STELLA | I'll never forgive your pathetic son, as long as I live. |
| JOHN | Please, Stella. Let's try and remain calm. |
| STELLA | Lucinda could have married any young farmer she wanted. |
| ALF | One thing's for sure, she'd have been quite at home feeding the pigs. |
| LUCINDA | That's done it, Mummy. I can feel the tears welling up. |

*(Lucinda starts crying again)*

| | |
|---|---|
| STELLA | How dare you. |
| ANNE | I believe the forecast is good for the next few days. |
| STELLA | If only Lucinda had chosen someone more suited to our lifestyle. |
| JOHN | Are you trying to say that Jason's not good enough. |
| STELLA | You couldn't possibly deny there's a difference in their upbringing. And that explains why that rotten maggot son of yours couldn't face up to his responsibilities. |
| SID | You were right, John, when you said she was a jumped-up tart. |
| STELLA | I beg your pardon? |
| SID | John only said the other day, if it wasn't for your husband's money, you'd be making a living on the streets. |
| STELLA | WHAT! How dare you! Take that! |

*(Stella throws drink at Sid)*

| | |
|---|---|
| ANNE | Mind you, these weathermen never get it right. |

*(Alf defends himself with the microphone pole)*

**49**

| | |
|---|---|
| ALF | Don't get your knickers in a twist. |
| STELLA | *(Stella kicks Alf. He starts hopping around room)* You pea-brained oaf. |
| ALF | Ahh ... That hurt. You vicious old bag. |

*(Stella grabs the mayor's picture from the sideboard and smashes it over Alf's head. The picture finishes up with Alf's head poking through it)*

| | |
|---|---|
| STELLA | Oh dear. I've just shattered the mayor's work of art. |
| ALF | Sod the mayor. You nearly shattered my brains. |
| LUCINDA | Mummy, please. *(Lucinda is still crying. The Rev. Stevens enters from hall)* |
| FRED | *(Trying to hold Stella)* Calm down, Stella. |
| REV. STEVENS | Hello, everyone. Goodness me. *(Nobody spots the Rev. Stevens)* Stop, children, please stop. |

*(There is a bell on sideboard which the Rev. Stevens picks up and rings loudly)*

We must love one another.

*(Everybody stops fighting and looks at Rev. Stevens. Alf removes picture and throws it on sideboard)*

| | |
|---|---|
| STELLA | Hello, Vicar. How nice to see you. |

*(Stella brushes Fred off. A photo falls from his pocket)*

| | |
|---|---|
| REV. STEVENS | You've dropped a photo, Mr Stubble. *(Rev. Stevens picks up photo and looks at it. Then he has another close look)* It's you, Mrs Parsons. Um ... you're almost overexposed. |
| STELLA | I beg your pardon? |
| REV. STEVENS | The photo, you're well-developed. I mean, what natural colour. |
| STELLA | *(Looking at photo)* It's my holiday snap. What are you doing with it? |

*(Stella snatches photo and puts it into her handbag)*

| | |
|---|---|
| FRED | It ... er ... must have fallen into my pocket the other day. |
| REV. STEVENS | I've just called to see what's happening about the wedding. |
| ALF | What wedding's that, Vicar? |
| LUCINDA | That's it, I'm off again. *(Lucinda starts to cry again)* |
| REV. STEVENS | Is there any news? |
| ANNE | Not yet. But I'm sure there will be. |
| REV. STEVENS | Should I cancel the choir, and tell the organist? |

| | |
|---|---|
| STELLA | No. Just iron your cassock and make sure your organ's working. The wedding's going ahead as planned. |
| REV. STEVENS | Just supposing Jason hasn't returned by then? What are ...? |
| STELLA | Reverend Stevens, I'm telling you, and everybody here, Jason will marry Lucinda. Even if they have to take him up the aisle in a straitjacket. |
| REV. STEVENS | Let's hope that won't be necessary. |
| STELLA | I've spent the last year organising my daughter's wedding, and it's not being ruined by some irresponsible bridegroom. Come on, Lucinda, let's go. |

*(Lucinda gets up still whimpering. Stella glares at Sid and Alf)*

| | |
|---|---|
| | I'll see you all at the church. On Saturday. |
| FRED | Let's hope Jason turns up. |
| STELLA | If he doesn't turn up for his wedding, I'll still see you in church for his funeral. |

*(Stella and Lucinda exit to hall, followed by Anne)*

| | |
|---|---|
| SID | Her husband deserves a medal. *(To Rev. Stevens)* May I give you our card, Vicar? |

*(Sid gives Rev. Stevens a card)*

| | |
|---|---|
| REV. STEVENS | Thank you. |
| SID | From the cradle to the grave. We can help you relive life's treasured moments. |
| ALF | Stereophonic sound's extra. But we knock off the V.A.T. for cash. |

*(Anne enters room)*

| | |
|---|---|
| ANNE | Would you like a cup of tea, Vicar? |
| REV. STEVENS | No, thank you. I just popped in for a progress report. |
| ANNE | I'd better have your phone number in case we hear anything. |
| REV. STEVENS | Well ... um ... I'm out most of the time. I'll ring you tomorrow. *(Pause)* Goodbye. |

*(Rev. Stevens exits to hall)*

| | |
|---|---|
| ANNE | What are we going to do? I've never seen Stella so angry. |
| ALF | I'll have a bruise on my leg. *(Alf pulls up his trousers and puts his leg on sofa arm. He starts rubbing his leg)* I might do her for GBH. |
| SID | She really went berserk. This was one of me best shirts. Look at it now. |
| ALF | I don't fancy your Jason's chances when Stella gets hold of him. |

| | |
|---|---|
| ANNE | I just want him to come home, so we can sort things out. |
| SID | Why don't you put an advert on the local radio? |
| ALF | Yeah, they're always finding missing dogs. |
| SID | *Missing, Jason, slipped his lead, friendly and ready to be mated. If found before Saturday, take him to the church. If found after Saturday, put him in the dog-house.* |

*(Sid, Alf and Fred laugh)*

| | |
|---|---|
| ANNE | It's nothing to laugh about. Whatever does he think he's playing at? |
| FRED | He'll come back when he's ready. I must be going. I've promised to help at the 'Nag's Head.' |

*(Fred walks to hall exit)*

| | |
|---|---|
| SID | We'll come with you. |
| ALF | I could do with a brandy, purely for medicinal purposes. |

*(Alf rubs his leg)*

| | |
|---|---|
| SID | You will let us know what's happening, won't you? Only our services are in great demand. |

*(Sid, Alf and Fred exit to hall)*

| | |
|---|---|
| ANNE | I'll never be able to show my face again. |
| JOHN | Don't worry. Things are never as bad as they seem. |
| ANNE | No, I suppose you're right. I mean the fact that Stella spent thousands of pounds, plus the last year organising the grandest wedding this town's ever seen, and our son, who happens to be the bridegroom, decides to do a last minute disappearing act. It's no big deal! |
| JOHN | Now you've put it like that, when I get my hands on Jason, I'll kill him! |
| ANNE | I owe you an apology for thinking you fancied Stella. When Fred dropped her photo, I realised what had happened. |
| JOHN | He's certainly one for the girls. And Stella desperately craves affection. |
| ANNE | If they ever get together, it'll be like a wrinklies' version of Romeo and Juliet. |
| JOHN | I'm going to check my roses. It might help me relax. |

*(John exits to kitchen. Anne tidies up room)*

| | |
|---|---|
| VOICE ON CB | *Road Hog* to *Ice Maiden*, have you got your ears on? |
| ANNE | *(Looking around room)* Pardon? |

| | |
|---|---|
| VOICE ON CB | *Road Hog* to *Ice Maiden*, have you got your ears on? Come back. |
| | *(Anne walks over to the C.B. and looks at it)* |
| | I've got an eyeball on Jason, shall I give him a good slapping? |
| ANNE | No, don't do that. Leave the boy alone. |
| VOICE ON CB | *Ice Maiden*, come back. |
| | *(Anne grabs CB and piece of paper, she presses button on CB)* |
| ANNE | This is *Ice Maiden* to *Road Hog*. *(Looking at paper)* That's a negatory, don't hurt him.. |
| VOICE ON C.B. | That's a big ten four. He's heading home. I'll call off the truckers. |
| ANNE | That's good. *(Looking at paper)* I mean, that's a big Roger Dee, over and out. |
| | *(Anne puts down CB, runs to kitchen exit and shouts from door)* |
| | John, come here quickly. |
| | *(John enters)* |
| JOHN | Whatever's wrong? |
| ANNE | *Road Hog*'s said Jason's on his way home. Oh, I'll explain later. *(Doorbell rings)* That's probably him. |
| | *(Anne exits to hall)* |
| | *(Off)* Stella, Lucinda. |
| | *(Anne, Stella and Lucinda enter)* |
| STELLA | I've forgotten my CB. *(Pause)* Is there any news? |
| ANNE | *(Looking suspicious)* Um … No, not a thing. We've just been sitting here talking. *(Looking vague)* About the … weather. |
| STELLA | I'll give Reg another call, to see if there's been any sightings. |
| | *(Stella gets hold of C.B.)* |
| ANNE | No, you musn't do that. *(Pause)* He's just called and … said … umm … he'd gone for a tea break. |
| STELLA | Oh … all right. I'll try him later. |
| | *(Stella puts CB in her handbag)* |
| LUCINDA | Do you think Jason will come back, Mummy? |
| STELLA | Of course he will, darling, if he wants to carry on living. |
| ANNE | We must go to the supermarket, John. |

**53**

| JOHN | *(Looking vague)* Sorry? |
|------|------|
| ANNE | The supermarket, you know we were just going to get the shopping. |
| JOHN | What? ... Oh yes, sorry to rush you, Stella. |
| ANNE | We'll let you know the minute we hear anything. |

*(Doorbell rings)*

Oh, no ... How's Reg been keeping?

| STELLA | I beg your pardon? |
|------|------|
| ANNE | Your Reg. He's such a hard-working man, is he keeping well? |
| STELLA | Yes, thank you, although he'll be a lot better when we've sorted out this wedding. |
| ANNE | Ah, yes, the wedding. |
| JOHN | When we got married, it rained all day. We all looked like drowned rats. The photographer's camera was full of water. |

*(Doorbell rings again)*

| STELLA | How very interesting. Aren't you going to answer the door? |
|------|------|
| ANNE | Just going. John, why don't you show Stella and Lucinda your roses. |
| JOHN | Oh yes. Come with me, they're out in full bloom. |

*(John beckons Stella and Lucinda to kitchen exit)*

| STELLA | We haven't got time now. |
|------|------|

*(Stella and Lucinda walk to hall exit. Anne runs in front of them)*

| ANNE | Are you sure? John said they'll definitely win first prize at the flower show. |
|------|------|
| STELLA | *(Unconvincingly)* I'm so thrilled for you. |
| JOHN | I've got a hundred quid bet riding on them. |

*(Doorbell rings again)*

| STELLA | Would you please let us out and that persistent bell pusher in. |
|------|------|
| ANNE | I think I'm going to have a nervous breakdown. |
| STELLA | I suggest you have it after we've gone. |

*(Anne exits to hall)*

| ANNE | *(Off)* Oh, it's you. Come in. |
|------|------|

*(Anne and Chris enter)*

What a lovely surprise, it's Chris, I'm so pleased to see him. He's such a good friend of the family.

**54**

*(Anne kisses Chris, he looks surprised)*

| | |
|---|---|
| STELLA | Have you heard anything? |
| CHRIS | No. I just called to see if you'd got any news. |
| STELLA | Are you sure, you're not hiding anything? |
| LUCINDA | Don't get on at Chris, Mummy. It's not his fault. |
| STELLA | Umm … these boys are all the same. It's probably got something to do with their upbringing. |
| ANNE | I'm sure Chris would tell us if he knew anything. |
| STELLA | I wouldn't bet on it. |
| ANNE | Well, we mustn't hold you up, Stella. |
| STELLA | No, I must be going. I've got to co-ordinate the search. |
| ANNE | Keep us informed if you hear anything. |
| JOHN | Bye, Stella, Lucinda. |

*(Stella and Lucinda go to hall exit. Doorbell rings)*

| | |
|---|---|
| ANNE | Good grief, this is like Russian Roulette. |
| STELLA | It would probably save time if I answered the door. |

*(Stella exits to hall and returns holding Jason by the ear)*

Look what I've found. *(Looking very angry)* Before you have a chance to make one of your speeches, let me tell you and everyone here, you will be marrying my Lucinda on Saturday. Make no mistake about that!

## ∽ *Curtain* ∽

55

# ACT II

## ∽ Scene II ∽

*(As the curtain rises, Anne is walking around room and John is sitting in a chair)*

ANNE    It should have been the happiest day of his life. He never smiled once. *(Pause)* He was forced into it and it's all your fault.

JOHN    Amazing, isn't it. If anything goes wrong, it always turns out to be my fault.

ANNE    You should have stopped the wedding. You're his father, you could have done something.

JOHN    What, like shoot the vicar?

ANNE    Don't be stupid. You should have sorted something out.

JOHN    Not even an Act of God would have stopped it.

ANNE    Jason only got married because he couldn't let Lucinda down on her big day.

JOHN    I think the fact that Stella was going to kill him had some bearing on his decision.

ANNE    He was in an impossible situation.

JOHN    It was the grandest wedding I've ever been to. The whole town was at a standstill. Even the mayor was impressed.

ANNE    I heard Stella telling *him* that Reg goes out Friday nights.

JOHN    I'll say one thing for Stella. Where men are concerned she never gives up.

ANNE    At least you're off her hit list now, after stinking out the church with rotting manure.

JOHN    How was I to know that idiot farmer would deliver it fifteen minutes before the wedding, blocking our car up the drive.

ANNE    You should have put your wellies on. Or at least taken your suit off.

JOHN    There wasn't time. I was sweating when I'd finished.

ANNE    You don't have to tell me. I was in the fall-out zone.

**56**

| | |
|---|---|
| JOHN | Still, at least I had plenty of room when I was eating my meal. |
| ANNE | What are we going to do about Jason? |
| JOHN | It's too late now. He's made his vows, for better or for worse. |
| ANNE | I feel sorry for him. He won't have that 'special feeling' you get when you're first married. |
| JOHN | What 'special feeling'? |
| ANNE | I should choose your next words very carefully. They could be your last. |
| JOHN | Don't get me wrong – I'm happy enough. *(Pause)* Well, for a married man. |
| ANNE | I can't believe I'm hearing this. |
| JOHN | All I'm saying is that as the years pass, it can get a bit monotonous. |
| ANNE | What are we talking about? Your performance in bed? Because that's just about as exciting as watching paint dry. |

*(Doorbell rings. John exits to hall)*

| | |
|---|---|
| JOHN | Saved by the bell. *(Off)* Hello, Fred, come in. |

*(John enters, followed by Fred wearing earrings)*

| | |
|---|---|
| FRED | It's a sad time for Jason, losing his freedom. It must be a black day for the boy. |
| ANNE | What makes you men think that you're doing women a favour by marrying them? |
| JOHN | Yes, well, umm ... what did you think of the reception? |
| FRED | It was all very nice. Well, as far as I can recall. |
| JOHN | Fred, you're wearing earrings. *(Pause)* They're a bit over the top, aren't they? |
| FRED | Actually they're not mine. I'm looking after them for a lady friend I met at the wedding. |

*(Anne looks closely at the earrings)*

| | |
|---|---|
| JOHN | So who's this mystery woman? |
| FRED | I can't remember. I'd sunk a lot of beer by the end of the day. Everything was a blur. |
| ANNE | They look very familiar. |
| FRED | I was on my way home. It was so dark I couldn't see a thing. Anyway, I came across this woman. She was well slaughtered. |

**57**

| | |
|---|---|
| JOHN | Most of the guests were. That was probably because the drink was free. |
| FRED | We were just having a bit of a snog, when suddenly she went into overdrive. I think she may have bruised me tonsils. Here, come and have a look. *(Fred opens his mouth widely. John has a look in)* |
| ANNE | All right, Fred, we get the picture. |
| FRED | She gave me her earrings so we could get down to some real serious ... |
| ANNE | I don't think we want to hear any more. |
| JOHN | Speak for yourself. I do. Tell us exactly what ... |
| ANNE | And you've no idea who it was? |
| FRED | No, it was pitch-black. In any case I was well shot away. |
| ANNE | So why are you wearing them? |
| FRED | I'm trying to find their rightful owner. |
| ANNE | I think that's a very responsible attitude, Fred. |
| FRED | Actually, I couldn't care less who owns them. I just want another snog, now I'm sober. It's about time I had a bit of female company to spice up my life. |
| JOHN | Fred, come and have a look at my roses. They're ready for the flower show next week. I'll be walking off with first prize. |

*(Fred and John exit to kitchen. Anne tidies up. The phone rings, Anne picks it up.)*

| | |
|---|---|
| ANNE | Hello ... Oh hello, Bill, ... thank you very much, he'll be pleased. I'll pop round with him. I've got some photos to show you ... see you in a minute ... Bye. |

*(Anne puts down phone and continues tidying up. Doorbell rings, Anne exits to hall)*

*(Off)* Hello, Stella, come in.

*(Stella and Anne enter)*

| | |
|---|---|
| STELLA | What a day, it was definitely the best wedding this town's ever seen. |
| ANNE | It all went very well. I should think you were very pleased. |
| STELLA | I just couldn't believe she was my little girl. |
| ANNE | I must say Lucinda looked lovely. |
| STELLA | Like a princess, waiting for her knight in shining armour. |
| ANNE | I thought the bridesmaids were sweet. |
| STELLA | My Lucinda was like a pure white angel, ready to ascend into Heaven. |
| ANNE | The choir sang well, no sign of laryngitis. |

**58**

| | |
|---|---|
| STELLA | My Lucinda was like a film star. I'm surprised no-one asked for her autograph. |
| ANNE | The weather couldn't have been better. |
| STELLA | My Lucinda was like a beauty queen who'd just won the title. |
| ANNE | Would you like a coffee? |
| STELLA | My Lucinda looked like ... Oh, no thank you. |
| ANNE | I expect you're glad it's all over. |
| STELLA | The wedding may be over, but people will talk about it for years. All the local papers were there. Did you hear the interview on the radio? |
| ANNE | No, I'm afraid we were fighting our way through manure at that point. |
| STELLA | The mayor's invited me for drinks next week. He's introducing me to our local MP. |
| ANNE | I'm so pleased for you. (Pause) It was very kind of you to pay for the honeymoon. |
| STELLA | Think nothing of it. They'll enjoy Scotland. I wanted them to go abroad, but Lucinda doesn't like flying. |
| ANNE | What time are they travelling? |
| STELLA | Their train leaves at two-fifteen this afternoon. It was far better for them staying locally last night. |
| ANNE | You shouldn't have booked them into the Grand. It's so expensive. |
| STELLA | Reg uses it all the time for his business clients. |
| ANNE | I've never been in there. |
| STELLA | We treat it like a second home. I've told Lucinda to mention my name. That'll keep them on their toes. |
| ANNE | You must be very pleased with everything. |
| STELLA | We've had a few unnecessary hiccups, but it's been a fairy tale ending. I suppose you could say I'd organised the perfect wedding. |
| ANNE | I'm pleased to see that success hasn't gone to your head. |
| STELLA | Of course, you can't hold me responsible for those two imbeciles who videoed the wedding. |
| ANNE | I thought they did very well. |
| STELLA | If I never see either of them again, it'll be too soon. |
| ANNE | I'm sure you'll be pleased with the tape. |

**59**

| | |
|---|---|
| STELLA | That's most unlikely. *(Pause)* You didn't find any earrings at the reception, did you? I seem to have lost mine. |
| ANNE | Were they *(Anne gives a description of earrings Fred is wearing)?* |
| STELLA | Yes, how did you know? |

*(Fred and John enter from Kitchen)*

| | |
|---|---|
| JOHN | Hello, Stella. |
| ANNE | *(To John)* Bill rang, we've got to slip next door for a minute. |
| JOHN | What does he want to borrow now? |
| ANNE | He doesn't want anything. He's got a special feed for your roses. Apparently it's used by professional growers. |
| JOHN | Oh ... I've always said he was a good bloke. |

*(Anne picks up some wedding photos, then looks at Stella)*

| | |
|---|---|
| ANNE | Let's pop round and get it. Fred'll look after you Stella. |

*(John and Anne exit to hall)*

| | |
|---|---|
| STELLA | Did you enjoy the wedding, Mr Stubble? |
| FRED | I certainly did, how about you? |
| STELLA | It was like a dream come true. *(Pause)* You're wearing earrings. *(Stella looks very closely)* Where did you get them? |
| FRED | At the reception, someone gave them to me to look after. |

*(Stella removes earrings from Fred's ears)*

| | |
|---|---|
| STELLA | These are my earrings. |
| FRED | Oh!! *(Pause)* So you were the girl I met on my way home. |
| STELLA | Good grief, it's all coming back to me. |
| FRED | It was so dark I didn't recognise you. |
| STELLA | I seemed to be in a daze, I was just floating along on a cloud. |

*(Stella puts earrings in her handbag)*

| | |
|---|---|
| FRED | I'm not surprised, the amount of drink you'd put away. |
| STELLA | I gave you the earrings to look after. Then we ... |
| FRED | Er ... yes ... we did, didn't we? Well I never, what a funny old world it is. |
| STELLA | I hope you don't think I was throwing myself at you? |
| FRED | You certainly know how to Rock and Roll. |
| STELLA | I beg your pardon? |

| | |
|---|---|
| FRED | I was watching you on the dance floor. You looked lovely at the wedding. You're like a bottle of wine. *(Pause)* You improve with age. |
| STELLA | Thank you, Fred, you're a real gentleman. |
| FRED | You'll be lonely without Lucinda. |
| STELLA | Yes. And Reg is always working. |
| FRED | He shouldn't leave a good-looking woman like you on her own. |
| STELLA | Oh, Fred. *(Stella gets close to Fred)* You say the nicest things. |
| FRED | I've just bought a CB. I call myself *Silver Fox*, why don't you pop round and see it. |
| STELLA | Reg goes out Friday nights. I get so bored on my own. |
| FRED | Come round this Friday and I'll show you my equipment. |
| STELLA | I'll be there. *(Stella gets her handbag)* I've got something for you. *(Stella gets out her holiday photos)* Here, it's yours. *(Stella hands Fred photo)* |
| FRED | *(Looking at photo)* I'll put it under my pillow, it'll warm me up on cold winter nights. |
| STELLA | I've just had a thought. Reg has just got himself a very lucrative continental contract. |
| FRED | Oh, that's nice. |
| STELLA | No, you're missing the point. He'll soon be away several days travelling through Europe. You'll be able to come over to my house. We're very private. |
| FRED | Sounds good to me. |
| STELLA | I thought after Lucinda left, life would be dull, but it looks as though it's on the up again. |
| FRED | Yeah, you could be right. I've managed to get a few of them Viagra pills. |
| STELLA | I've always fancied the more mature man. |
| FRED | Youngsters haven't got the monopoly on life's sensual pleasures. It's just that we're built for comfort and they're built for speed. |
| STELLA | I'm all for a bit of slow cruising. |
| FRED | I suggest you fasten your seat-belt, I'm already firing on all cylinders. |
| STELLA | *(Getting hold of Fred's hand)* Oh, Fred. Thank you for bringing some life back into my life. |

*(They start to kiss. Doorbell rings. Fred puts photo in his pocket)*

| | |
|---|---|
| FRED | Oh damn. I'll go. *(Fred exits to hall)* |
| | *(Off)* Hello, Sid, Alf. |

**61**

| | |
|---|---|
| STELLA | Oh no, I don't believe it. |

*(Sid, Alf and Fred enter, Sid has videotape and camera, Alf has a microphone)*

| | |
|---|---|
| SID | It's a masterpiece! Although I say it myself, it's absolutely brilliant. |

*(Sid holds up videotape)*

| | |
|---|---|
| | Fades and wipes, camera angles correct. Superb editing. Stereophonic sound. Still, we won't bore you with all the technical details. |
| ALF | We've worked through the night. I've given it my all. I'm completely drained. |
| SID | How many copies do you think you'll want? |
| STELLA | I'm not sure, I'll need to see it first. *(Aside)* Thank goodness we've got lots of photos. |
| SID | There won't be any illegal pirates, will there? |
| STELLA | *(Looking confused)* I beg your pardon? |
| SID | We own the copyright. Additional tapes must be supplied by us. |
| STELLA | If you say so. *(Aside)* I shouldn't think we'll be wanting any. |
| ALF | Has anybody heard what happened to the best man? |
| FRED | It's unlike Chris. He's normally so reliable. |
| STELLA | I knew he couldn't do the job. I told them he wasn't up to it. |
| FRED | There wasn't any sign of him all day. I wonder whatever made him disappear like that? |
| STELLA | He probably couldn't face up to his duties. Making a speech would be difficult for someone like him. |
| SID | Poor old Jason looked completely lost. |
| STELLA | He should never have chosen that Chris. I knew he wasn't suitable for such an auspicious occasion. |
| ALF | Who was the boy you got to stand in? |
| STELLA | One of Lucinda's young farmer friends, he's got innate breeding. |
| ALF | Is that catching? |
| STELLA | There's certainly no chance of you getting it. |
| ALF | That's good. *(Looking at Sid)* You can't be too careful nowadays. |
| STELLA | I thought his wit and charm really made the day. |
| ALF | I suppose he's one of them yippies. |
| SID | You mean yuppies, Alf. |

**62**

| | |
|---|---|
| ALF | Yeah, that's what I said. |
| FRED | Had Jason ever met him before the wedding? |
| STELLA | No, he went straight from boarding school to university. Now he's into organic farming. |
| ALF | He should be careful messing about with things like that. It ain't natural. |
| FRED | I will say he did very well. |
| SID | Perhaps Chris thought the wedding would be cancelled if he didn't turn up. |
| STELLA | He should have realised what I start I always finish. |
| ALF | I enjoyed the reception. |
| STELLA | *(Unconvincingly)* I'd like to say it was a pleasure having you. |
| ALF | It was good in that tent. |
| STELLA | I assume you're referring to the marquee? |
| ALF | That band was good. I'm sure some of them blokes could read music. |
| STELLA | They could all read music. They're a professional orchestra. *(Pause)* I'll tell John you're here. |

*(Stella exits to hall)*

| | |
|---|---|
| SID | Her Reg didn't say a word at the reception. He was like a fish out of water. |
| ALF | I caught him on video, phoning one of his drivers. During the vicar's prayers. |
| SID | They say he's a workaholic. |
| FRED | He certainly doesn't enjoy socialising, and a little bird's told me he's lost his libido. |
| ALF | Was it valuable? Because he could always claim off his insurance. |
| FRED | I was on about his testosterone levels. |
| ALF | *(Looking vague)* Yeah, so was I. |
| SID | I'd like to find out who let the tyres down on our dolly. It ruined all our mobile shots. |

*(Stella enters from hall)*

| | |
|---|---|
| STELLA | They're just coming. |
| SID | I see the place next to you is for sale. I've always fancied living in a country cottage. |
| STELLA | *(Aside)* Thank goodness it's way above your price range. |

**63**

*(John and Anne enter from hall, John is carrying a container)*

JOHN        That's the first thing he's ever given me. Hello, Sid, Alf. I won't be a minute, I've got to get this feed on my roses.

*(John exits to kitchen)*

ALF         It's a wrap.

ANNE        I beg your pardon?

ALF         It's in the can.

ANNE        I'm sorry, Alf, you've lost me.

STELLA      They've finished the video.

SID         It'll probably bring tears to your eyes.

STELLA      *(Aside)* I'm sure it will.

ALF         We've worked non-stop to get it finished.

SID         We'll be able to relax tonight. I fancy going to the 'Nag's Head'.

ALF         Your husband certainly enjoyed himself the last time he was there. He had a real good night with that erotic dancer.

ANNE        Erotic dancer?

ALF         At Jason's stag-night, didn't he tell you?

ANNE        He hasn't said anything.

ALF         They were like a double act. *(Pause)* By the time he'd finished, she was as naked as a jaybird.

FRED        He only did it to try and cheer Jason up. *(Aside)* Shut up.

ANNE        Is there anything else I should know?

ALF         If you've got a spare hour, I'll fill you in on all the juicy bits.

*(Phone rings, Anne answers it)*

ANNE        Hello … Good grief! … Oh no!

*(Anne puts down phone and runs through kitchen exit)*

STELLA      What was all that about?

ALF         Perhaps it was that erotic dancer asking John to join her act.

FRED        Will you shut up about her. Are you trying to get John hung?

ALF         Have I said something wrong?

FRED        Oh, no. You should have videoed them. Then Anne could have watched every explicit detail.

**64**

| | |
|---|---|
| ALF | I never thought of that. |

*(Anne enters helping John in, he is clutching the watering-can with both hands and he looks numb)*

| | |
|---|---|
| ANNE | Sit down, you'll be all right in a minute. |
| SID | Whatever's up with him? |

*(Anne sits John down in a chair, he is still clutching watering can)*

| | |
|---|---|
| ANNE | He's just sprayed weedkiller over his prize winning roses. |
| ALF | What did he do that for? It won't do them any good. |
| ANNE | Bill, next door, got the packets mixed up, he gave John weedkiller by mistake. *(To John)* Let go of the watering-can, dear. |
| JOHN | I'll kill him. He did it deliberately. |
| ANNE | Don't be so stupid, of course he didn't. |

*(John gets up out of chair and goes to hall exit)*

| | |
|---|---|
| JOHN | Why have we been lumbered with the neighbours from hell? I'm going to blow his house up. |
| ANNE | John, come here. |

*(Anne pulls John away from door and tries to remove watering-can from his hands)*

| | |
|---|---|
| | It was an accident. |
| JOHN | I'm going to the garden centre tomorrow. |
| ANNE | It's too late to get any roses for the show now. |
| JOHN | No, I'm buying some ten-foot conifers to plant all down our boundary. If he wants war, he can have it. |
| ANNE | I'll get you a drink. |

*(Anne sits John back down still holding watering-can. Anne pours a drink and gives it to John)*

| | |
|---|---|
| | Here you are. |

*(John puts watering-can down and has a drink)*

| | |
|---|---|
| JOHN | I can't believe it. My head's thumping. |
| ANNE | Oh dear. It could be a bit of blood pressure. *(Pause)* Caused by Lusty Linda's naked body. |
| JOHN | Who's Lusty Linda? |
| ALF | I've just told your missus about that erotic dancer, and her pet python. |
| JOHN | You've lost me. |

**65**

| | |
|---|---|
| ANNE | Sorry dear, am I making things too complicated for you. I'M TALKING ABOUT THAT STRIPPER YOU ASSISTED IN GETTING STARKERS. |
| ALF | The one you said you'd like to ... |
| JOHN | Thanks Alf, I owe you. *(Pause)* It was just a bit of harmless fun. |

*(John has another drink)*

| | |
|---|---|
| SID | Would you like us to video your roses in all their magnificent splendour? |
| ALF | Before they all drop dead. |
| JOHN | Well, I suppose it's better than nothing. |
| SID | Right, leave it to us. |

*(Sid and Alf exit to kitchen, walking like two undertakers)*

| | |
|---|---|
| JOHN | My head's a bit better now. |
| ANNE | Don't speak too soon, the pain could return. |

*(Anne picks up a large vase)*

| | |
|---|---|
| JOHN | There's no need to be like that. |

*(Jason and Lucinda enter from hall. Lucinda looks lovely. She is now very self-confident and talks without her lisp)*

| | |
|---|---|
| | This is just not my day. |
| JASON | Are you all right, Dad? |
| ANNE | Yes, he's all right. He's just sprayed his ... Jason! Lucinda! |

*(Anne puts down vase)*

| | |
|---|---|
| STELLA | WHAT ARE YOU DOING HERE? You should be at the station. |
| ANNE | Jason, why aren't you on honeymoon? |
| FRED | Perhaps he's had enough of married life already. |
| JASON | That's just it, we're not married. |
| ANNE | } |
| STELLA | } WHAT? |

*(Stella drops down onto sofa)*

| | |
|---|---|
| ANNE | Is this your idea of a joke? Because if it is I don't find it at all funny. |
| JASON | It's not a joke, Mum, we don't understand what's going on either. |
| STELLA | How can you say you're not married? That doesn't make any sense. *(Getting hysterical)* Two hundred and fifty people were at your wedding. We've got dozens of photos; I watched you sign the register. |

| | |
|---|---|
| LUCINDA | Mum, I know all this. If you remember, I was the bride. |

*(Stella gets up and starts to pace up and down the room)*

| | |
|---|---|
| STELLA | This is a nightmare. Please tell me I'm dreaming. |
| FRED | Just calm down a minute Stella, we'll soon ... |
| STELLA | Calm down! What do you mean calm down? |
| JOHN | Let's find out what's going on. Jason, tell me exactly what's happened? |
| JASON | After the reception we went to the hotel. |
| LUCINDA | At breakfast this morning the manager gave us this note. |

*(Jason removes a piece of paper from his pocket and reads it)*

| | |
|---|---|
| JASON | *Please return home immediately, you are not married. I will explain everything at eleven-thirty* and it's signed the Reverend Stevens. |
| LUCINDA | The manager told us the note was left by a vicar. |
| ANNE | Why would he leave a note saying you're not married? |
| JOHN | If you don't get to the station soon, you're going to miss your train. |
| LUCINDA | There's no point going on honeymoon if we're not married. |
| FRED | She's quite right. It's bad enough if you are married. |
| ANNE | And you didn't see the Reverend Stevens? |
| JASON | No. He'd left before we'd got up. |

*(Reverend Stevens enters)*

| | |
|---|---|
| REV. STEVENS | Hello, I'm glad you're all here. |

*(Stella runs over to the Rev. Stevens and grabs him)*

| | |
|---|---|
| STELLA | What do you mean by telling my daughter she's not married? |
| REV. STEVENS | If you'd just bear with me, I'll explain everything. |
| STELLA | This had better be good. Your life depends on it. *(Stella lets go of Rev. Stevens)* |
| REV. STEVENS | I knew Jason didn't want to get married. |
| JASON | Who told you that? |
| FRED | *(Aside)* He probably had a message from God. |
| REV. STEVENS | I also knew Stella wouldn't cancel the wedding. |
| STELLA | You seem to be well informed. But that doesn't explain anything. |
| REV. STEVENS | I had to do something. How could I let my best friend marry the wrong girl? |

| | |
|---|---|
| JASON | Best friend? *(Rev Stevens removes wig, glasses, collar and cassock)* <u>CHRIS</u>! |
| LUCINDA | I can't believe it. |
| STELLA | Good grief! |
| ANNE | Whatever's going on? |
| FRED | Now I've seen everything, including a reverend being defrocked. |
| CHRIS | When Jason and I were young we made a pact. If either of us was in trouble, the other would do anything to help. |
| STELLA | So what's this stupid pact got to do with my daughter's wedding? |
| CHRIS | Jason was desperately trying to stop the marriage. |
| JASON | I'd begged Chris to help me. |
| CHRIS | I'm sorry, Lucinda, but I had to do something, so I decided to become the Reverend Stevens. |
| STELLA | You'll be sorry all right, you'll be very sorry. |
| ANNE | I don't understand any of this. |
| CHRIS | After Jason told me about Julie, I went home. My mum's church warden and she'd just had the news about the Reverend Hall breaking his legs. |
| STELLA | It won't be just your legs I'll break, it'll be every bone in your body. |
| CHRIS | That's when I had this flash of inspiration. |
| STELLA | You'll have a flash of my hand round your head any minute. |
| LUCINDA | Mum, for once in your life, please be quiet. |
| CHRIS | I decided with the Reverend Hall in hospital, I'd take his place. |
| ANNE | Take his place? What are you talking about? |
| CHRIS | Vicars are like policemen. The uniform gives them an air of authority, which makes people listen. |
| FRED | That's quite true. Last week a copper got my full attention when he threatened to book me, for speeding. |
| CHRIS | Anyway, I got a wig and cassock and dressed up. I was hoping to convince Lucinda that the marriage was a mistake. |
| JASON | But when you got here, she'd already left. |
| CHRIS | Yes, I saw you with Julie. Then I knew I had to stop the marriage. |
| JASON | I never recognised you. |
| CHRIS | That's when I realised I could get away with it. |

**68**

| | |
|---|---|
| STELLA | I've had enough of this silly chatter. I'm phoning the police. *(Walking to the phone)* |
| FRED | Hang on a minute, Stella. Let the boy finish. |
| ANNE | So why didn't they send a proper vicar? |
| CHRIS | Mum was dealing with the arrangements. I intercepted her calls from the Dean's office. |
| STELLA | May God forgive you, I certainly won't! |
| CHRIS | I'd convinced everyone that I was the replacement vicar sent to officiate. |
| JOHN | So why go ahead with the wedding? |
| CHRIS | Because I realised I couldn't stop it. *(Pause)* Stella wanted a magnificent wedding; she had one. Jason didn't want to be married; he isn't. |
| STELLA | You've made a mockery of the sanctity of marriage. |
| CHRIS | You're wrong. I've prevented a mockery from taking place. |
| STELLA | I suppose you think you're clever. Let me assure you, you're going to pay for this. |
| JASON | How did you know what to do? |
| CHRIS | As a choirboy I'd watched dozens of weddings. |
| | *(They all stand silent for a few seconds)* |
| LUCINDA | So we're *not* married? |
| CHRIS | No, I'm sorry Lucinda, you're not. |
| STELLA | You're in big trouble, boy. Impersonating a vicar is a very serious offence. I'm phoning the police. They'll lock you up and throw away the key. |
| | *(Stella picks up phone)* |
| LUCINDA | No, Mum, don't do that. |
| | *(Lucinda puts phone down)* |
| STELLA | Why ever not? What's up with you, Lucinda? |
| LUCINDA | I'm pleased we're not married, it would never have worked. |
| STELLA | Have you gone completely mad? |
| LUCINDA | Yesterday, I realised the marriage was a mistake. We spent all last night talking. |
| ANNE | *(Looking at John)* This is all your fault, you should have explained about the birds and the bees. |
| JASON | It's got nothing to do with the birds and the bees, but it's got everything to do with being in love. |

**69**

| | |
|---|---|
| LUCINDA | Mum, I've spent my whole life living in your shadow. Now I'm going to do my own thing. |
| STELLA | This is all too much for me. How can I ...? |
| FRED | I think your daughter's just grown up, Stella. It's time to let her go. |
| LUCINDA | Jason, I'll always look on you as the brother I never had. |

*(Lucinda kisses Jason)*

| | |
|---|---|
| CHRIS | *(To Lucinda)* I'm sorry, it was never my intention to hurt you. Perhaps we could have a drink some time? |
| LUCINDA | I'd love that. Jason's very lucky having such a good friend. |
| CHRIS | I think he's crazy to finish with such a gorgeous girl. |

*(Chris stands by Lucinda. They look into each other's eyes)*

| | |
|---|---|
| STELLA | I'm not feeling very well. It's all going to start again with another one of these no-hopers. |

*(Sid and Alf enter)*

| | |
|---|---|
| SID | Hello, Chris. *(To Jason)* Why aren't you two on honeymoon? |
| JASON | It's a long story, but we're not married. |
| ALF | Yes you are. We've got it all on video. |
| JASON | Chris made a guest appearance as the vicar. |
| CHRIS | Because I married them, they're not married. |
| ALF | I don't understand any of that. |
| SID | Don't strain your brain, Alf. *(Pause)* What about our video? |
| STELLA | Throw it in the bin where it belongs. *(Stella hands over video)* |
| SID | But we've spent hours getting it ready. It's probably the best one we've ever made. |
| STELLA | You keep it. I certainly don't want it. |
| SID | *(To Lucinda)* When you find the right boy, don't forget to let us know. We're the professionals. |
| LUCINDA | I'll bear that in mind. *(Lucinda looks at Chris)* |
| STELLA | I don't ever want to see you two clowns again. *(Pause)* I've never been so humiliated in all my life. |
| FRED | Calm down, Stella. It could have been worse. |
| STELLA | Are you joking? I've just organised the biggest marriage that never was. |
| JOHN | Look on the bright side. One day you'll be able to do it all again. |

| | |
|---|---|
| CHRIS | Mum phoned the bishop's office this morning and told them what I'd done. |
| STELLA | I feel positively sick. Whatever will the mayor say? I'll be a laughing stock. |
| | *(Doorbell rings. John exits to hall)* |
| JOHN | *(Off)* Hello, you'd better come in. |
| | *(John and Julie enter)* |
| JULIE | Hello, Jason, why aren't you on your honeymoon? |
| JASON | Because I'm not married. |
| JULIE | Aren't you? *(Looking happy)* You're not? Oh, that's wonderful ... I mean ... |
| CHRIS | That's why I left you the message to call round. *(Pause)* Jason'll explain everything. |
| | *(Julie talks to Jason)* |
| LUCINDA | I hope you'll be very happy together. |
| JASON | Thank you. |
| LUCINDA | I've just had a brilliant idea. *(Looking at Chris)* What are you doing this week, Chris? |
| CHRIS | Nothing really ... why? |
| LUCINDA | Come to Scotland with me now. There's a first class hotel booked and waiting. I need to get away for a while. |
| CHRIS | What! ... I mean ... I'd love to. |
| LUCINDA | Come on then. Let's go and get you packed, or we'll miss the train. |
| STELLA | But you can't. You're a married ... |
| LUCINDA | No I'm not, Mum. *(Giving Stella a hug)* Thanks for a lovely wedding, even if I didn't get married ... Bye. |
| | *(Lucinda holds hands with Chris and they run to hall exit)* |
| STELLA | I'm not feeling very well. *(Phone rings, John answers it)* |
| JOHN | Hello ... Yes, I'll get him ... Sid, it's your wife. |
| | *(John hands phone to Sid, he talks in background)* |
| JULIE | Why are all those reporters out the front? |
| ANNE | They must have found out what's happened. |
| STELLA | This isn't the sort of publicity I was looking for. |
| JOHN | I think this is one wedding we'll never forget. |

*(Sid puts down phone)*

SID      My wife said the phone's not stopped. We've had television companies, video shops, lots of townsfolk, all wanting copies of the wedding tape.

STELLA      That's just typical. Why can't people mind their own business?

*(Sid holds up video tape)*

SID      This little baby's going to be a big earner for us. *(Sid puts his arm on Alf's shoulder)* We'll never be able to thank you enough, Stella.

STELLA      Thank me? What for?

SID      If it hadn't been for your daughter's reception, I wouldn't have seen that cottage next to you is for sale.

STELLA      What are you getting at?

SID      Well, when we've sold all your wedding videos, we'll have enough money to put a deposit on it. Looks like we're going to be neighbours.

STELLA      WHAT! I CAN'T TAKE ANY MORE.

*(Sid and Alf walk over to Stella to shake hands. She faints)* Ahh ...

*(Stella collapses into a chair. Anne, John, Fred, Sid and Alf try to revive her)*

JASON      *(To Julie)* Will you marry me?

JULIE      I'd love to. *(Pause)* On one condition. Let's make absolutely certain that Chris is the best man this time.

*(Jason and Julie kiss passionately)*

# ❧ *Curtain* ❧

To Bob.                    12 May 2000

   Very many thanks for all
your help.
              Ray

# THERE GOES THE BRIDE

## Raymond Hopkins

Farcical Comedy         ISBN: 185205 250 3                    M6 F4

Jason Taylor, a quiet unassuming person, is one week away from marrying Lucinda, his childhood sweetheart. The overzealous bride's mother, Stella Parsons, has turned the wedding into a personal crusade. No expense has been spared and a year's preparations have all come together to make it the event of the decade. Lucinda, who has always been dominated by her mother, has gone along with the lavish arrangements. As the wedding looms ever closer, everything is on track. That is, until Julie, a girl from the local florists, calls at the Taylors' to make some final arrangements. By a twist of fate, Jason is at home alone. Their inevitable first meeting sparks off that magical chemistry which makes two people fall hopelessly in love. From that point on, the plot twists and turns in a frantic manner, making the wedding a far more memorable occasion than even Stella could have imagined. Another hilarious play by the author of the highly successful LOVE BEGINS AT FIFTY.

---

# LOVE BEGINS AT FIFTY

## M3 F6     ISBN: 185205 229 5

A modern farce in two acts by Raymond Hopkins

### SOME PRESS OPINIONS

This is one of the most frenetically funny farces I have reviewed for some time, up to the standards of the best of Ray Cooney ... side-splitting laughter ... a fast and furious farce which provides hilarious opportunities.

THIS WAS ONE OF THE SUMMER SHOWS IN TORQUAY IN 1999 WHERE IT PLAYED TO RECORD-BREAKING AUDIENCES THROUGHOUT A THREE MONTHS' RUN

---

SEND FOR OUR CATALOGUE OF OVER 300 TITLES

# HANBURY PLAYS

Keeper's Lodge, Broughton Green, Droitwich
Worcestershire WR9 7EE
01905 23132 – Phone and Fax